The Maccioni Family Cookbook

The Maccioni

Photographs by *Elizabeth Zeschin*

Family Cookbook

Egi Maccioni with Peter Kaminsky

STEWART, TABORI & CHANG · NEW YORK

Published in 2003 by
Stewart, Tabori & Chang
A Company of La Martinière Groupe
115 West 18th Street
New York, NY 10011

Export Sales to all countries except Canada,
France, and French-speaking Switzerland:
Thames and Hudson Ltd.
181A High Holborn
London WC1V 7QX
England

Canadian Distribution:
Canadian Manda Group
One Atlantic Avenue, Suite 105
Toronto, Ontario M6K 3E7
Canada

Library of Congress Cataloging-in-Publication
Data

Maccioni, Egidiana.
The Maccioni family cookbook / Egi Maccioni
with Peter Kaminsky ;
photographs by Elizabeth Zeschin.
p. cm.
ISBN 1-58479-288-4
1. Cookery, Italian—Tuscan style. 2. Maccioni,
Egidiana. I. Kaminsky, Peter. II. Title.
TX723.2.T86M33 2003
641.5945´5—dc21   2003054210

The text of this book was composed in
Hoefler Type Foundry Requiem.

Designed by Jim Wageman

Printed in Singapore

10 9 8 7 6 5 4 3 2 1

First Printing

Contents

Foreword Mario, Marco & Mauro Maccioni

FOR OUR MOM, AS FOR ALL ITALIANS, cooking is first and foremost a matter of ingredients rather than recipes. Purity, simplicity, and perfection of ingredients inspire her. Even when combining ingredients in traditional ways, she always adjusts them to the seasons and her creative impulses.

We learned the lesson of ingredients at an early age. When we came home from elementary school we'd smell the delicious sauce that was simmering on the stove and ask what was for dinner. And she would answer, "sugo alla come mi pare," which means "sauce my way." This meant if there were no tomatoes around, then maybe she used porcini with some pancetta because those were the best ingredients. Rather than specific recipes, it is much truer, when speaking of cooks in the Italian home kitchen to speak of the influence of people. We remember food by the way our Aunt Clara or our grandmothers would make a meal. The same is true for any of the generations of Italian women who fed their families the same way Mama fed ours: Start with the ingredients then add inspiration and memories of the cooks who have influenced you.

Mom would let us help in her kitchen, whether it was the small kitchen in our New York apartment or the larger one at our Italian home in Tuscany where we went each summer. We would stir, bang the pots, mess up the counter, drop things on the floor, and Mom would laugh, encourage us, and make excuses to our Dad if we woke him from his Sunday nap. Joining in the cooking was part of being Italian. Though we grew up as New York kids, we were always reminded of our Italian heritage. We learned to speak the language, make the food, and most of all, enjoy the meal.

The generosity of spirit and hospitality of the Italian kitchen carried over into our restaurants. In the beginning, running the restaurants was Dad's department, while Mom was in charge of guarding the Italian traditions of the kitchen that made our restaurants stand out from other fancy, formal places. Dad loved Mom's food and sought to bring it to fine dining, and we boys wanted to grow up to be like Dad in the dining room with a lot of Mom's passion in the kitchen.

Now that we are grown up and restaurateurs in our own right, Mom has joined us in running our restaurants, including the one that most reflects her spirit and our Tuscan traditions, Osteria del Circo. But in every Maccioni restaurant you will find her signature dishes, such as bollito misto and ricotta and spinach ravioli.

Through all those childhood afternoons, helping her in the kitchen, listening to her sing in her beautiful voice as she cooked, we learned to eat like Tuscans, and we became a restaurant family that keeps its tradition of cuisine and hospitality. Whether in the home or the restaurant, those are two good things to have at any table. We're happy that Mama is finally sharing the wonderful dishes we grew up with and love to this day.

introduction

Introduction

I COME FROM A SMALL TOWN IN TUSCANY. It has very good food. You could say the same about any town in my region. There is something about Tuscany that awakens the appetite and sharpens it. Maybe it is the clear clean air that carries the scent of cooking fires. Or maybe the fields that produce the sorana, the world's most delicate bean. Or the orchards full of apples and pears. Or the hills and forests with wild mushrooms that we pick in the fall when the fires from burning grapevines and the scent of freshly pressed grapes fill the air with an irresistible perfume.

Mostly, though, it is the people. In a region blessed with great ingredients, yet where people have always had to work so hard to make a living, food was always the centerpiece of daily life, the one chance for families to get together and share their experiences. This was true of my hometown, Montecatini. It is a small city halfway between Florence and the sea. Not much has happened there and it would probably be as unknown as hundreds of other beautiful little Tuscan towns were it not for the hot springs.

Since the time of the Etruscans and, after them, the Romans, the mineral waters of the springs of Montecatini—Tettuccio, Regina, Rinfresco, Toretta, and Tamerici—have been a prime attraction. Toscanini came to the beautiful spa at the Grand Hotel and La Pace Hotel. So did the Duke and Duchess of Windsor, Orson Welles, Audrey Hepburn, Deborah Kerr, Gina Lolabrigida, and Clark Gable.

It was a glittering spot in its time. My husband worked at La Pace Hotel in his very first job, just starting on the path that would take him and me to America and the glittering Le Cirque, where we drew on our experience at that great hotel in Montecatini as we served our food to stars, political leaders, royalty, and everyday (but demanding) New Yorkers. It has been an exciting journey.

Today, just as it was when I was a little girl, our favorite foods are the simple, delicious, and economical recipes that every Tuscan family enjoys. The cuisine of common people has always been economical because that was the only way they could survive. When I was very young this was never truer.

I was born in the Great Depression, a time of hardship that continued until the end of the Second World War. Many things that I later took for granted were very hard, almost impossible to find. No butter, no sugar. I didn't see my first banana until I made a trip to Rome when I was eight or nine. No chocolate either. At the end of the war, I remember the American GIs coming through Montecatini, throwing chocolate bars from their jeeps and tanks. I can still see my first chocolate, a Hershey bar in a brown and white package, tumbling in the air toward me. And then the wonderful M&Ms in their little tubes—so colorful, like a rainbow of lentils I thought (that's what the candies reminded us of, so we called them lentils).

Although my father was a baker we rarely had any white flour, which is doubly hard on an Italian family that loves pasta. With the little that we had, I would follow my Nonna Augusta through the neighborhood. She would go from house to house with her rolling pin under her arm and I would go with her. We would go into someone's kitchen and make tortellini and tagliatelle right there.

Since food was more valuable than money people paid us with a little flour, some sugar, maybe some butter. Nonna Augusta taught me to make the tortellini around my pinkie so that they would be nice and small. I was so little I could hardly reach the table!

During the worst days of the war, the farmers had no one to pick their crops, so their fields and orchards were often full of ripe fruits and vegetables. My great aunt, Genoveffa, and my mother, who was a tiny woman, would take a wheelbarrow and trek into the fields. Once they came back with twenty watermelons. Another time it was bushels of pears. After these expeditions we had a diet of watermelon, watermelon, and more watermelon, followed by a diet of pears, pears, and pears. We couldn't be picky eaters when food was so hard to come by.

Somehow, we managed. There were chestnuts to gather on the hillsides. Fat porcini mushrooms in October. Sometimes my Uncle Giorgio would come back from hunting with a few rabbits in his bag. Those rabbits had to feed a lot of people. In our home we had my grandma

LEFT TO RIGHT:

ME AT 10 YEARS
OLD CLIMBING
THE GATES OF THE
TORETTE BATHS

MY MOTHER
OUTSIDE OF THE
TORETTE BATHS

MY FATHER

and grandpa, her sisters, my uncles and aunts, my parents and me, the only child until my brother was born when I was 14. The Italians dote on children and, being the only child in a house full of Italians with a lot of love to give, I had a childhood that was very rich if you count your riches by the amount of love and attention you get.

Still, you can't eat love so every meal had to be stretched to the maximum. If the ingredients were scarce, time, skill and ingenuity were plentiful. Wonderful things came out of that kitchen with the Three Old Ladies, my Bolognese nonna, Augusta, and her sisters-in-law Livia and Genoveffa, gossiping, laughing, cooking and correcting each other's recipes all day!

And of course, not to forget my Tuscan grandmother, Leonella. Every time I went to visit her, the house was filled with the aroma of olive oil, sage, rosemary, garlic, and chunky, Tuscan-style potatoes. That was one of the first recipes I ever mastered.

I learned to treasure every one of those recipes. Where other families passed down lands, bank accounts, titles . . . the recipes were our heritage. My husband and sons and I have built a very successful family of restaurants, but whether we are cooking for the pope or the president, a billionaire or a newlywed, the menus always include the pastas and sauces, the bakery treats, the sausages and slow-braised recipes of my Italian childhood.

America, my new home, has come to mean something sweet and precious to me. And it is with that same feeling that I offer back to you the food that my family eats to this day. These are not "chef's recipes" with expensive hard-to-find ingredients and complicated time-consuming steps. This is a book of everyday recipes from a Tuscan mother.

I begin with the recipes of my childhood, simple food that formed the basis of my taste and my cooking. In the following section, I pick up the story when I became a young woman and fell in love for the first time with a dashing young man, Sirio Maccioni. Like me, he came from a humble background and he loved the gutsy food of the countryside. Then from all of our years together, there are a number of dishes that I always know will get him eating with gusto no matter how hard the day has been, and I include them here.

Next, as a mother of three, I had a table full of hungry boys each with the mysterious likes and dislikes of all children. One thing was for sure, though, they would learn their Italian heritage at our dinner table, and so I have put together a whole section of recipes that pleased my children and which I know will please yours, at least some of the time—and that's all a mother can hope for. Finally, in the course of our thirty-something years as restaurateurs Sirio and I, and now our boys too, have always included our Tuscan heritage on all of our menus. So now I offer to you our Tuscan dishes, which have always been loved by American diners.

May they serve your family well.

recipes from a tuscan

childhood

Pappa al Pomodoro *(Tomato Stew)*

LEONELLA WAS my Tuscan grandmother. I also had a Bolognese grandmother, Augusta. Leonella, though, was the one who cooked the most. I used to go over to see Nonna Leonella in her house with a beautiful rose garden. Leonella always made this soup. As with many of the most wonderful Tuscan recipes this one was made with bread that was leftover from the day before. Rather than throwing away the bread or feeding it to the pigeons she used it to add body to soup. For the Pappa al Pomodoro, you soak the bread and then squeeze out the water before adding it to the soup. My father, Bruno, was a proud Tuscan baker and he insisted, "you cannot make bread soup if it's not Tuscan bread!" He was right—up to a point—Tuscan bread is rough-textured and holds its body in a way that store-bought bread does not. Still, I have been making this with American bread since I came to New York and my four "boys" (my husband and three sons) love it. I've included my recipe for Tuscan Peasant Bread if you want to bake your own and have the Pappa al Pomodoro be really authentic.

Tuscan Peasant Bread

2 1/4-ounce envelopes active dry yeast
2 cups lukewarm water
3 1/2 cups all-purpose flour, unbleached if possible

1/2 cup whole-wheat flour
pinch salt
pinch sugar

In a large bowl, dissolve the yeast in 1/2 cup of the warm water. When it is thoroughly dissolved, add the remaining 1 1/2 cups warm water and mix well. Slowly stir in the flours, salt, and sugar until a heavy dough forms. Gradually stir in a little more flour if the dough is too sticky to handle.

Knead the dough until satiny smooth. Turn out the dough onto a floured board, cover with a clean towel, and let rise in a warm spot for about 1 hour, until it has doubled in bulk.

Preheat the oven to 400 F. Lightly grease a baking sheet or pizza pan and set aside.

Punch down the dough, and shape it into a round or oblong loaf. Place the loaf on the prepared baking sheet and bake in the middle of the oven until light brown and very crusty, 60 to 75 minutes. Transfer to a rack to cool completely before serving.

Makes 1 loaf.

Stew

½ pound Tuscan bread (about half a loaf) cut into
    ½-inch thick slices
1 quart cold water
½ cup olive oil, plus more for drizzling
1 pound chopped tomatoes (about 2 cups)
1 large onion, minced
1 small carrot, peeled and finely chopped

1 stalk celery, finely chopped
¼ cup chopped fresh parsley
20 large basil leaves, julienned, plus more leaves
    for garnish
1 cup hot water
salt
pepper

In a large bowl or dish, soak the bread slices in the cold water until they are soft, about 20 minutes to 1 hour, depending on how dry the bread is.

In a large saucepan, heat ½ cup of the olive oil over medium-high heat. Add the tomatoes, onion, carrot, celery, parsley, and basil and cook until the vegetables begin to soften, about 5 minutes.

Drain the bread well. Squeeze it to get rid of as much water as possible. Discard the water. Crumble the bread into the vegetables and stir well. Add the hot water, cover, and simmer for about 25 minutes, stirring occasionally.

Season with salt and pepper to taste. Serve the stew warm in individual bowls with a little drizzle of olive oil and a fresh basil leaf on top of each.

NOTE: If you are unable to find fresh, ripe tomatoes, you can substitute canned. Or you can add 2 tablespoons tomato paste with the tomatoes to increase the color and flavor of the dish.

Serves 6.

Ribollita *(Tuscan Bread Soup)*

BASICALLY, A MINESTRONE (vegetable and bean soup) with leftover bread. Ribollita is a one-bowl meal. There were so many things that went into this soup. It always caught my attention when I was a little girl. When I was five, Nonna Leonella decided I was old enough to hold a knife and start chopping alongside her. I would cut myself sometimes, not seriously, but enough to teach me to be cautious with tools. Leonella never cut herself, not even once.

1 pound dried white beans

2 quarts water

2 red onions, peeled and coarsely chopped

3/8 cup olive oil

1 clove garlic, coarsely chopped

2 tablespoons tomato paste dissolved in 1/2 cup water

1/2 head Savoy cabbage, cleaned, cored, and coarsely chopped

1 head black cabbage (also called Tuscan kale or cavolo nero), cleaned, cored, and coarsely chopped

1 bunch Swiss chard (about 10 leaves and stems), coarsely chopped

2 potatoes, peeled and cut into 3/4-inch cubes

1 stalk celery, coarsely chopped

2 carrots, peeled and coarsely chopped

1 small bunch fresh basil (about 3 sprigs), coarsely chopped

1/2 loaf Tuscan bread (about 3/4 pound), cut or broken into small chunks

extra-virgin olive oil, for drizzling

salt

pepper

Soak the beans overnight in the water. Drain the beans, reserving 6 cups of the water.

In a large soup pot, cook the onions in the olive oil on medium-high heat for 2 to 3 minutes. Add the garlic and cook for 2 minutes more.

Stir the diluted tomato paste into the onions and garlic. Add the cabbages, Swiss chard, potatoes, celery, carrots, basil, and the water reserved from the beans. Cover, and cook for 30 minutes, stirring occasionally. Add the beans and cook until soft for 5 to 10 minutes. Remove from the heat. Add the bread and mix well. Cover and let rest for at least 15 minutes before serving. Season with salt and pepper to taste. Serve in bowls with generous amounts of olive oil drizzled on top. (It is even better the next day, reheated.)

NOTE: Black cabbage can be difficult to find in the United States. I have had the most luck finding it in Chinese markets here. In this dish, you can substitute green cabbage or Savoy cabbage.

Serves 8.

Tuscan Fried Potatoes

WHENEVER I VISITED LEONELLA I would say "Nonna, can you make me some Tuscan fries?"
They were so good, maybe better than any other because they were my grandmother's.
The secret is taking a long time to make them so they get soft on the inside and crusty
and flavorful on the outside.

1 ½ cups olive oil

4 medium yellow potatoes, peeled and cut into wedges

4 cloves garlic, finely chopped

1 sprig fresh rosemary, or 1 teaspoon dried

1 teaspoon salt

pepper

Heat the olive oil in a large, heavy skillet over high heat until hot. Add the potatoes, garlic, rosemary, and salt. Spread the potatoes out in a single layer. Cook for 5 minutes on high heat, turning the potato wedges once to cook both sides. Reduce the heat to medium and cook the potatoes, stirring and turning occasionally, until crispy golden brown, about 25 minutes. Carefully remove the potato wedges to a platter covered with paper towels. Season with pepper. Serve immediately.

Serves 4.

Stracciatella

PERHAPS my oldest food memory is being awakened by a commotion in the kitchen while it was still dark out. It was Nonna Augusta.

"What are you doing Nonna?" I asked. "It's four o'clock in the morning."

"I'm making stracciatella for your uncle because he is going hunting and he needs something nutritious."

Then she would grind some nutmeg and whisk it into the pot to finish off the soup. Uncle Giorgio, in his high boots and heavy green wool would tromp into the room and wolf down a huge bowl of freshly made stracciatella. It must have done the trick because he would come home with pheasant, pigeons, doves, all kinds of wild birds. I loved to eat them, but as the junior member of the family I also had to pluck them, which was not my favorite job.

1 quart chicken broth

2 eggs

1/4 cup grated Parmesan cheese

2 tablespoons bread crumbs

pinch ground nutmeg

pinch salt

pinch pepper

In a small soup pot or saucepan, bring the broth to a vigorous boil over high heat.

In a small bowl, whisk together the eggs, Parmesan cheese, bread crumbs, nutmeg, salt, and pepper. Pour the batter into the boiling broth. Let all the bits of batter rise to the top of the broth, 3 to 5 minutes. Remove from heat and serve immediately.

Serves 4.

Minestrone

Mom was a master of psychology in getting us kids to help her in the kitchen.

"Who's brave enough to chop the onion?" she would challenge, knowing that one (or all) of us would answer,
"I'm big enough, Mama, I'm not going to cry!"

And then on through the carrots, the celery and so on. Once in a while there was a little bit of clanging when
Mom allowed us to play drums on the pots, so it wasn't all chop, chop, chop.

— MARCO

½ cup extra-virgin olive oil

½ pound Savoy cabbage (about ½ of a small head)

1 large red onion, peeled and sliced

4 medium zucchini, cut into ¼-inch cubes

3 potatoes, peeled and cubed (about 1 pound)

2 stalks celery, finely chopped

2 large carrots, peeled and finely chopped

1 clove garlic, finely chopped

1 thick slice prosciutto (about ⅛ pound), cut into
    ½-inch pieces

2 quarts hot chicken broth

1 small bunch parsley (about 10 sprigs), coarsely chopped

1 small bunch basil (about 10 sprigs), coarsely chopped

4 small tomatoes, cubed

1 pound fresh pinto beans (or ½ pound dry)

1 small bunch Swiss chard (about 10 leaves), stems
    removed and leaves coarsely chopped

1 small bunch spinach (about ¼ pound), coarsely
    chopped

⅔ cup pasta, rice, or 3 slices Tuscan bread

salt

pepper

In a large soup pot, heat the olive oil on medium-high heat. Add the cabbage, onion, zucchini, potatoes, celery, carrots, garlic, and prosciutto and cook until all the vegetables are well-coated and begin to soften, about 5 minutes. Add the hot stock, parsley, basil, and tomatoes and bring to a boil. Reduce heat and simmer for 45 minutes. Add the pinto beans and cook for 30 minutes. (If using dried beans, see Note below.) Add the Swiss chard and the spinach, and cook for 2 minutes longer, until the greens are fully warmed in the soup.

If you are using pasta or rice, cook it as directed on its package. If you are using Tuscan bread, toast it until golden brown, and break it into large croutons.

Just prior to serving, add the pasta, rice, or croutons. Season with salt and pepper to taste. Serve hot.

NOTE: Put the dried beans in a large saucepan. Add 2 cups of water and bring to a boil. Boil for 2 minutes. Cover and let sit for 1 hour. Drain.

Serves 6.

Semolino Soup

Nonna Augusta would make this body-warming soup for major holidays such as Christmas or Epiphany or Easter. Epiphany was my favorite because that was the day we youngsters would get presents. Of course, during the hard times of the war the presents weren't very grand but to a young girl they were still something to look forward to as much as my boys dreamed about their bicycles and boom boxes. I particularly remember one year I had a well-used little doll. We hung it over the fireplace and my mother said, "La Befana [Mother of the Epiphany] will make it all new." Next morning, when I awoke, my doll had a new dress and a freshly painted face. Alongside were presents of tangerines and dried fruits which were the best treats in those days.

Croutons

3 eggs
1/3 cup Cream of Wheat
1/3 cup grated Parmesan cheese
6 tablespoons butter, melted
1/8 teaspoon freshly grated nutmeg
salt
white pepper

Soup

2 small white onions, peeled
1/4 leek

2 quarts water
1/2 chicken (about 2 pounds, or less), skinned
1/2 pound beef
1 large stalk celery
1 carrot
1 pear or plum tomato, halved lengthwise
1 sprig parsley
1 sprig basil
2 teaspoons salt
4 peppercorns
1 chicken bouillon cube

For the croutons:
Grease a 10-inch, nonstick skillet. Preheat the skillet on medium heat.

In a small bowl, whisk together the eggs, Cream of Wheat, Parmesan cheese, butter, nutmeg, and salt and white pepper to taste until thoroughly combined. Pour the batter in the prepared pan. Cook slowly, until it turns golden. Flip over carefully with one or two spatulas, and cook the other side until deep golden brown. Transfer to a platter covered with paper towels. Let cool for 10 minutes or more. Then cut into tiny cubes.

FOR THE SOUP:

If you have a gas stove or grill, roast the onions and leek directly over the flame until they begin to turn brown and just a little bit burned on the outside. Set aside. Otherwise, omit this step.

Bring the water to boil in a large soup pot. Add the leek, onions, chicken, beef, celery, carrot, tomato, parsley, basil, salt, and peppercorns. Let boil for 1 hour. Strain the soup, reserving the broth. (Discard the remainder, or use the beef and chicken for Polpette, see recipe on page 29.)

Return the broth to boil. Add the bouillon cube and stir to incorporate it into the broth. Add the croutons. Let simmer for 1 minute. Serve immediately.

Serves 6.

Pizza with Mushrooms and Cheese

My father, Bruno, was a marvelous baker. Pizza, focaccia, and pastries all came out of his oven perfectly done. I guess I inherited my pizza-making ability from him, and my sons have picked it up from me. Pizza was always a Sunday afternoon project in the Maccioni home in New York. The boys had fun helping Mama (and covering themselves and the kitchen in flour). We would make the dough, then I would put in it a warm place to rise while we went out for a walk. When we came home, it was always up to me to finish the job because the boys were on to other things.

Pizza Dough

2 ½ cups all-purpose flour
1 cup lukewarm water

1 ¼-ounce envelope active dry yeast
1 teaspoon olive oil

Combine all the ingredients in a food processor. Mix just until well combined and no more. Place dough in an oiled bowl or on an oiled baking sheet. Cover with a clean kitchen towel. Place in a warm, draft-free spot. Let rise until the dough has approximately doubled in bulk, 30 minutes to 2 hours.

Punch down the dough and divide in half. Form a ball with each half and follow pizza recipe.

Makes dough for two 13-inch pizzas.

12 or more dried black wild mushrooms, preferably those imported from Italy
Pizza Dough (see recipe above)
salt

4 cups thinly sliced fresh mushrooms (about 1 pound)
2 cups grated mozzarella cheese (about ½ to ¾ pound)
pepper
¼ cup olive oil

Put the dried mushrooms in a small bowl and cover with warm water. Let sit for ½ hour or more, until the mushrooms soften.

Place each ball of pizza dough in the center of an oiled 13-inch pizza pan (or large baking sheet). Using lightly floured fingers, pat each ball into a thick round, about 8-inches across.

Drain the water from the softened mushrooms. Shred them into small pieces. Scatter the pieces over the rounds of pizza dough. Sprinkle lightly with salt. Scatter the fresh mushroom slices on top of each pizza. Using your fingers, press the mushrooms into the dough while you push out the dough to cover the entire pizza pan (or to make a 13-inch circle if using a baking sheet). Cover and let sit for $1/2$ hour in a warm spot.

Preheat the oven to 350 F. Scatter 1 cup grated cheese on top of each pizza. Sprinkle generously with pepper. Drizzle 2 tablespoons olive oil on top of each pizza.

Place the pans in the oven, and bake the pizzas until the cheese just begins to bubble, 15 to 20 minutes. Transfer the pans as close as possible to the bottom of the oven (the oven floor or the lowest rack). Bake for 5 minutes longer to crisp the bottom crust.

Serves 8.

MY THREE SONS: MARCO

Whenever we made pizza, Mom would tell us "I remember when your grandfather would make bread and he would spend the whole night kneading and letting it rise. He used to say that it was important to remember to put the top back on the olive oil bottle because the mice were so smart that if you left it open they would get your oil. They knew they couldn't fit their heads into the bottle so they would stick their tails in and then lick off the oil!"

Polpette (*Meatballs*)

WE DON'T use the word "leftovers" very much in Italian. Even in English it has a meaning of "not quite as good as freshly made." We think just the opposite. Many already made ingredients add character and depth to Polpette: bollito misto, a roast, cold cuts, beef, veal, chicken, and especially mortadella for extra flavor. I loved polpette as a little girl, and as a wife and mom in New York I could always count on all my guys snapping them up. Sometimes to make the polpette even softer I add a mashed boiled potato or two. Use my recipe here as a guide but remember this is not a precise recipe. It's the thing you do at home when you wonder what to make with the food in those Tupperware containers in your refrigerator.

¾ pound cooked chicken

¼ pound cooked beef

2 eggs

¾ cup grated Parmesan cheese

¼ pound ricotta cheese

3 ounces mortadella, peeled and broken up

1 slice white sandwich bread

2 tablespoons milk

1 tablespoon finely chopped fresh parsley

½ clove garlic, finely chopped

salt

pepper

½ cup fine bread crumbs

vegetable oil, for deep frying

In a food processor, combine the chicken, beef, eggs, Parmesan, ricotta, mortadella, bread, milk, parsley, and garlic. Pulse to the consistency of ground meat; do not puree. Season with about ½ to 1 teaspoon each of salt and pepper, or to taste.

Form approximately 1 tablespoon of the meat mixture into a round patty. Repeat with the remaining meat. Flatten the patties a bit on top and dip them in the bread crumbs to coat completely. Place the coated patties on a baking sheet. Cover with plastic wrap and refrigerate them for 1 hour.

Heat the vegetable oil in a fryer or deep pot until hot. Deep fry the patties until golden brown. Remove from oil and transfer to platters covered with paper towels. Serve warm.

NOTE: I often use the boiled meat from the Semolino Soup (see page 24) to make this dish. Serve with a little salad on the side.

Serves 6.

Pizza with Anchovies and Cheese

ALTHOUGH KIDS don't always love anchovies, I did and so did my boys. In Tuscany, our oven was so small that we usually left the pizza-baking to my father. He would make up the pizza at the bakery and bring it home. When my baby brother, Giacomo, was married, my father made twenty sheet pans of pizza and put them all together so that they looked like a pizza that was more than twenty feet long.

1/2 cup olive oil
Pizza Dough (see recipe, page 27)
8 anchovies or more, cut in half
1/4 cup capers
1 cup canned peeled tomatoes, well-drained and
   cut into 1/2-inch pieces

1 teaspoon dried oregano
salt
2 cups grated whole-milk mozzarella cheese
pepper

Pour 2 tablespoons olive oil into the center of each of two 13-inch pizza pans. Using lightly floured fingers, pat each ball if pizza dough into a thick round. Add one round of dough to the center of each pizza pan. Pat and press the dough to cover the bottom of the pans, rim to rim. Cover and let sit in a warm spot for about 30 minutes.

Preheat the oven to 350 F. Scatter equal amounts of the ingredients over each of the two pizzas in this order: anchovies, capers, tomatoes, oregano, salt to taste, cheese, generous amounts of pepper, and the remaining 1/4 cup olive oil.

Place the pans in the oven and bake the pizzas until the cheese begins to bubble, about 15 minutes. Transfer the pans as close as possible to the bottom of the oven (to the oven floor or the lowest rack). Bake for 5 minutes longer to crisp the bottom crust.

Serves 8.

MY THREE SONS: MARIO

We would help Mom make pizzas but now that I have three
children myself, I can appreciate how much "help" we really gave
and how much bother it must have been in reality. Three brothers,
three different sets of taste buds. I liked the anchovies or mushrooms,
Marco liked his plain, Mauro wanted more of the "American"
things that they put on pizza in school or the pizza shop. That
could be anything from pepperoni to pineapple. To make peace,
my mother would kick us all out of the kitchen, take a sheet pan
and put Marco's ingredients on one part, Mauro's on another
and mine on another.

Donzelle Fritte con Acciughe *(Fried Dough with Anchovies)*

DURING THE WAR, the Germans forbid us to listen to the radio (I guess they were afraid we would hear instructions from the Partisans who were seeking to overthrow them). Instead of surrendering our radio, one afternoon my mother, father, grandmother, and Uncle Renato carried the family radio—our treasure—up the hill in a "funeral procession," wrapped it and buried it. Four years later, we dug up the radio, brought it home, plugged it in, and when the music poured out of it we hugged, and cried, and danced for hours, stopping only to eat delicious morsels like these donzelle.

$^2/_3$ cup all-purpose flour
$^1/_4$ cup water
1 tablespoon olive oil
pinch salt

pinch sugar
2 ounces anchovies
10 leaves fresh sage
vegetable oil, for frying

Combine the flour, water, olive oil, sugar and salt in a food processor, and pulse just until it is well mixed. Cover the dough and let rest for 1 to 2 hours at room temperature.

Roll out the dough with a pasta machine or rolling pin until it is about $^1/_8$-inch thick. Cover one half of the sheet with the anchovies and sage leaves. Double the other half of the dough sheet over the first and roll out one more time. Cut the dough into diamond shapes.

Preheat the vegetable oil in a deep pot or deep-fry fryer. Add the dough diamonds and deep fry in the vegetable oil, turning once, until both sides are golden brown. Serve immediately.

Serves 4.

Insalata di Riso Estiva (*Summer Rice Salad*)

AUGUST IN MONTECATINI can be very hot, so hot that a salad is all you can think of eating. I try to avoid long-cooking oven meals. My Aunt Graziella, who was married to my mother's brother, Renzo, taught me this recipe. What goes into it depends on what you have on hand. For me, though, it needs artichokes, cold boiled rice, and anchovies. I love this. Sirio is indifferent, but if I make it with a lot of anchovies, he loves it!

1 cup rice
4 pear or plum tomatoes, sliced
6 marinated artichoke hearts, thinly sliced
1 6-ounce can tuna, drained
3 stalks celery, coarsely chopped
1 small bunch arugula, finely chopped
1/3 cup black olives, pitted and thinly sliced
4 large leaves romaine lettuce (or any other pale green lettuce), cut into small pieces

2 anchovies, broken into small pieces
2 tablespoons capers
3 basil leaves, coarsely chopped
3/4 cup olive oil or less
3 tablespoons red wine vinegar
salt
pepper
1 tablespoon mayonnaise (optional)

Cook the rice according to the directions on its package. Set aside to cool for at least 30 minutes.

In a large bowl, combine the tomatoes, artichokes, tuna, celery, arugula, lettuce, onion, anchovies, capers, olives, and basil. Add the rice and toss well to combine.

In a small jar, shake the olive oil, vinegar, and salt and pepper to taste. Add the mayonnaise to the dressing if you wish. Mix well.

Pour the dressing over the salad, a little at a time, tossing well to combine, just until you have added enough dressing to lightly coat all the ingredients.

Serves 4.

Cacciucco (*Fisherman's Soup*)

AMERICANS always have a hard time saying this for some reason; ka-choo-koh. This is the classic fisherman's soup of Tuscany. If you travel around the Mediterranean you will find that all the people of the sea have a recipe for extra little fish that they find in their net that they can't sell. In my childhood, Fridays were meatless and you could count on having cacciucco or baccalà. For years I would make this with whatever my brother Giacomo brought back from his fishing expeditions. But after a scary accident he had while scuba diving to make a film about an abandoned ship, he gave up the ocean and I contented myself with the fish in the market. Fish recipes don't always travel across borders, but this hearty soup has been on the menu at Circo from the day it opened.

$\frac{1}{4}$ cup extra-virgin olive oil

5 cloves garlic, coarsely chopped

1 small onion, peeled and finely chopped

2 carrots, peeled and finely chopped

2 stalks celery, coarsely chopped

1 leek, well cleaned and coarsely chopped

1 pinch crushed red pepper

2 cups white wine

5 plum tomatoes, coarsely chopped

1 cup canned tomatoes (8 ounces)

1 bouquet garni made with 2 sprigs fresh thyme, 8 leaves fresh basil, and 1 small bunch of parsley, tied in cheesecloth

$\frac{1}{2}$ pound squid, cleaned and sliced into rings

15 littleneck clams, thoroughly rinsed

2 lobsters, halved, cleaned, and chopped into 1-inch pieces

6 large shrimp, shelled and deveined

$\frac{1}{2}$ pound monkfish, cut into 1-inch pieces

$\frac{1}{2}$ pound snapper, cut into 1-inch pieces

1 pound mussels, cleaned, beards removed

$\frac{1}{2}$ cup chopped fresh parsley

salt

pepper

6 cloves garlic

6 thick slices Tuscan bread, toasted or grilled with olive oil

Heat the olive oil in a very large saucepan. Add the garlic, onion, carrots, celery, leek, and crushed red pepper and cook over medium-high heat until the garlic begins to brown. Add the wine, the fresh and canned tomatoes, and the bouquet garni, reduce the heat, and simmer, covered, stirring occasionally, until the tomatoes are very, very soft, about 30 minutes. Whisk well to break up all the tomatoes.

Add the squid to the soup. Simmer, covered, for 30 minutes. Remove and discard the bouquet garni. Add the clams, cover and simmer for 2 minutes. Add the lobsters and shrimp and cook for another 2 minutes. Gently add the monkfish and snapper and simmer uncovered until the fish are just cooked through, 5 to 10 minutes. Gently stir in the mussels and parsley. Cook just until the mussels open, 1 to 2 minutes. Season with salt and pepper to taste.

Cut the garlic cloves in half and rub the cut sides on the toasted bread. Serve the cacciucco immediately with the bruschetta.

Serves 6.

MY THREE SONS: MAURO

When we were growing up, we spent our summers in Montecatini and would often go to the beach, especially Viareggio, which made a different cacciucco from the red wine–based recipe from Livorno, farther south. In Viareggio they used white wine and more premium-market fish. There was one restaurant, "Da Bombetta," that made a spectacular version, very traditional and very garlicky. My mom makes it more Viareggio style. The lobster and shrimp are her New York additions. It costs more to make, but it is amazing to taste.

Risotto al Ragu (*Risotto with Meat Sauce*)

NONNA AUGUSTA learned this in her childhood in Bologna. It is a very rich risotto, the kind of thing we would have on Sunday. During the week we rarely ate rich food. We didn't have desserts either. But on Sunday were would have a nice rich meal, the kind that fathers and uncles like to sleep after. Most risottos start with an onion, wilted in the pan. However, because this one is mixed with a rich ragu—the classic Bolognese sauce—I leave out the onion. As a young girl I used to beg Nonna Augusta to let me help her. With risotto it was sometimes more work than I had in mind. "Come over here and keep stirring," she would tell me, "and don't move for twenty minutes."

1/2 cup olive oil

6 tablespoons butter

2 small red onions, peeled and finely chopped

1 stalk celery, finely chopped

1 carrot, peeled and finely chopped

1/4 pound ground beef

2 cups chicken broth, plus more if necessary

2 chicken livers, finely chopped

1/3 cup tomato paste

1/2 cup red wine

salt

pepper

2 cups arborio rice

grated Parmesan cheese, for serving

In a large saucepan, melt the butter in the olive oil on medium-high heat. Add the onions, celery, and carrot and cook until the onion begins to soften, 2 to 3 minutes. Add the ground beef and cook 2 to 3 minutes more until the meat begins to brown. Add 1 cup chicken broth, the chicken livers, tomato paste, wine, and salt and pepper to taste. Simmer for 10 minutes.

Add the rice and return to a simmer. Cook, stirring constantly, until the liquid has been absorbed.

In a separate saucepan, heat the remaining 1 cup chicken broth. Stir the hot broth into the risotto about 1/2 cup at a time, making sure the previous addition has been absorbed before adding more. Cook until the rice is al dente, about 25 minutes. Serve warm with grated Parmesan sprinkled on top of each serving.

Serves 6.

Coniglio Fritto (*Fried Rabbit*)

WE DON'T eat rabbit very much here in America, but in Tuscany it is one of our favorites. We eat it the way Americans eat fried chicken. We also feed it to convalescents and young children because it is lean, easily digestible, very delicate and full of protein.

Every year for Pasquetta (the day after Easter) my grandmother hired a horse and carriage to carry the meal and our best dishes up the hillside for a picnic. She would make fried rabbit, chicken tripe, ricotta ravioli. As a so-called treat she used to put me up on the horse but I never liked horseback-riding so I always made her take me down and I ended up walking with the grown-ups.

olive oil for deep frying, plus 2 teaspoons
¾ cup all-purpose flour
2 eggs

salt
about 1 ¼ to 1 ½ pounds rabbit, cut into
    small pieces

Preheat the olive oil in a deep pot or deep-fat fryer.

In a large bowl, whisk together ¼ cup of the flour, the eggs, 2 teaspoons olive oil, and a pinch of salt until smooth.

Put the remaining ½ cup flour on a plate. Dip the rabbit pieces in it to coat lightly. Then, dip the rabbit pieces in the prepared batter. Carefully transfer the pieces to the preheated deep-fryer. Begin with the oil as hot as you can get it without creating smoke, and fry the rabbit at this temperature for 5 minutes. Then cover the pan, reduce the temperature setting to low heat, and continue frying the rabbit for 20 to 25 minutes longer until it is a honey-gold color. Turn off the heat and transfer the rabbit pieces to a platter covered in paper towels. Generously salt the fried rabbit pieces and serve immediately.

Serves 4.

Fried Artichokes

On summer Sunday nights in Tuscany, families flock to the seafood restaurants on the coast. Viareggio, Forte di Marmi and all points in between are swarming with hungry vacationers and locals from nearby towns. The sweet summer air is full of the unmistakable tantalizing aroma of frying things. Inland we used to have our own non-seafood, *frittura*. My mother was a great fryer. She served up crisp batches of Fritto Misto alla Toscana: chicken, rabbit, sweetbreads, zucchini flowers, and artichokes. Though artichokes take a little practice to prep, I think you will agree it is worth it when your children ask for seconds on vegetables.

vegetable oil, for deep frying
1 cup all-purpose flour
$^1/_2$ cup beer
1 egg, lightly beaten

1 tablespoon olive oil
2 very small artichokes, trimmed, choke
    discarded, and cut into wedges
salt

Preheat the vegetable oil in a pot or deep fryer.

In a small bowl, whisk together $^3/_4$ cup of the flour and the beer, egg, and olive oil to make a batter. Set aside.

Put the remaining $^1/_4$ cup flour on a plate and dip the artichoke wedges in it to coat lightly. Dip the wedges in the beer batter. Carefully transfer the artichokes to the preheated deep fryer and deep fry them until they are deep golden brown.

Transfer the fried artichokes to a platter covered with paper towels. Season with salt to taste and serve immediately.

Serves 2.

Polenta

ALTHOUGH MANY PEOPLE think all Italians eat pasta all the time, this really isn't the case. In Tuscany we eat lots of bread, rice and polenta. Nonna Augusta was very fond of polenta. She would usually serve it with something stewed, especially rabbit. After she made the polenta but before it was served, she would put a towel on a big wooden board. Then she would put the polenta on top of the towel and wrap it up. The cloth would absorb the extra water in the polenta so that it was never soggy. The next day my grandmother would fry it, and I liked it even more.

1 quart water   1 cup yellow cornmeal
1 teaspoon salt   olive oil, for leftovers

Bring the water to a boil in a large, nonstick pan. Add the salt and reduce the heat to a simmer. Add the cornmeal very gradually and stir constantly and rapidly until thoroughly incorporated. Continue simmering, stirring frequently, until the polenta comes away cleanly from the sides of the pan, 20 to 30 minutes. Remove from the heat.

Drape a large, clean kitchen towel into a large bowl. Carefully transfer the polenta to the towel in the bowl. Let sit for 5 to 10 minutes. The towel will absorb some of the water from the polenta, and it should firm up a bit. Then, using the towel, lift the polenta from the bowl, and transfer the towel and polenta to a serving tray. Serve immediately.

NOTE: After the meal, leave any leftovers on the towel. Flip the edges of the towel on top of the remaining polenta to cover it. Put it in the refrigerator to chill and set overnight. The next day, transfer the polenta from the towel to a cutting board. Cut into 1/2- to 3/4-inch slices. Cook the slices in approximately 1 to 2 tablespoons olive oil in a nonstick pan until it begins to turn golden. Serve immediately.

NOTE: The leftover polenta can also be sliced and then grilled on an oiled grill.

Serves 4 with plenty for leftovers.

Streudel

MY DAD picked up this recipe when he worked in Germany. He and his brother went there for a few years in the Depression when he could no longer afford butter, sugar, chocolate, or any other staples of baking. One of the things he returned with was this streudel recipe, which he adjusted to the Italian style by adding pine nuts, which are used in many Tuscan pastries.

Filling

3 slices dry white bread
1 stick (4 ounces) plus 3 tablespoons butter
$\frac{1}{2}$ pound pine nuts
3 pounds apples, peeled, cored, and sliced
$\frac{2}{3}$ cup sugar
zest of 1 lemon
1 $\frac{1}{2}$ cups raisins

Pastry

3 cups all-purpose flour
1 stick (4 ounces) softened butter
3 eggs
pinch salt
pinch sugar
1 to 2 tablespoons water
4 tablespoons butter, melted
1 egg yolk, beaten

FOR THE FILLING:
Chop the bread in a food processor.

Melt the butter in a large saucepan on medium heat. Add the chopped bread and pine nuts, increase the heat to medium-high, and cook briefly, just until well coated with butter, 2 to 3 minutes. Add the apples and sugar and cook, mixing well, until the apples begin to soften, about 10 minutes. Remove from the heat. Stir in the lemon zest. Let cool for 15 to 20 minutes. Stir in the raisins. Set aside.

FOR THE PASTRY:
Using an electric mixer or food processor, combine the flour, butter, eggs, salt, and sugar and mix, adding just enough of the water to obtain a silky texture. Cover the dough and let rest for 2 to 3 hours.

Preheat the oven to 400°F. Grease a 13-by-9-inch baking pan and set aside. On a large work-space, spread a piece of heavy plastic wrap or parchment paper as long as the work surface. Divide the dough in half. Place half of the dough in the middle of the plastic wrap and roll it out about 15 inches wide and as thin and as long as you can stretch it without breaking the dough. (If a small hole forms, do not patch it, but make sure it will roll inside the strudel. If too many holes form, re-roll the dough.) Brush half of the melted butter on top.

Divide the filling in half. Sprinkle half of the prepared filling over the rolled out pastry, leaving a 1- or 2-inch border. Using the plastic or parchment to help you, lift up one end of the pastry, and roll it into a log. Tuck the edges under the log. Place the log on one side of the prepared pan, leaving room for the other log.

Repeat with the remaining pastry dough, melted butter, and filling, placing the second log alongside the first in the prepared pan.

Brush the egg yolk on top of the logs. Bake for 30 minutes. Then reduce the heat to 350 F, and bake until the strudels are deep golden brown and crisp, about 10 minutes longer. Serve warm.

Serves 8 to 12.

Torta di Riso (*Rice Cake*)

THIS IS A SIGNATURE Tuscan and Bolognese dish that my mother taught me. It was a special Sunday or holiday dessert. Here in America, I still keep the Italian custom of serving desserts only on Sundays and holidays. Sometimes, when we are dining at home, Sirio will ask me, "What's for dessert?" And I tell him, "Darling, this is not a restaurant. We have desserts on special days." And that's that.

2 ½ cups milk

¾ cup arborio rice

½ cup water

4 tablespoons butter

strips of zest from ⅓ lemon

strips of zest from ¼ orange

¼ cup bread crumbs

¼ cup all-purpose flour

2 ¼ teaspoons baking soda

1 ⅓ cups ricotta cheese, preferably fresh (about 10 ounces)

3 whole eggs, lightly beaten

3 egg yolks, lightly beaten

½ cup granulated sugar

⅓ cup heavy cream

3 tablespoons Sambuca or other anise-flavored liqueur

1 teaspoon vanilla extract

2 tablespoons melted butter

confectioners' sugar, for dusting

In a heavy saucepan, combine the milk, rice, water, butter, lemon peel, and orange peel. On medium-high heat, bring the mixture to a boil. Reduce the heat and simmer, stirring occasionally, until all the liquid has been absorbed, about 30 minutes. Remove the lemon and orange peel. Chop the peels finely and return them to the rice mixture. Remove from the heat and set aside to cool for at least 10 minutes.

Preheat the oven to 375°F. Grease a 12-by-8-inch baking pan. Coat with the breadcrumbs. Set aside. In a small bowl, combine the flour and baking soda. Set aside.

In a large bowl, combine the ricotta, whole eggs, egg yolks, sugar, and cream. Mix well. Add the flour mixture and mix well. Mix in the cooled rice mixture. Stir in the Sambuca and vanilla.

Spoon the batter into the prepared pan and spread evenly to cover the entire pan. Pour the melted butter on top. Bake in the preheated oven until the top is golden brown and it does not jiggle when you shake the pan, 30 to 40 minutes. Remove from the oven and let cool for 1 hour. Dust the top lightly with confectioners' sugar. Cut into squares or diamonds. Serve warm, room temperature, or chilled.

Makes 24 2-inch squares.

Torta di Ricotta *(Ricotta Cake)*

ALTHOUGH MY DAD was the professional when it came to baking, my mother had some wonderful desserts including this ricotta cake, which she made for my first Communion when I was seven years old. For that special occasion my mother made the most beautiful dress for me out of antique lace from a church altar. Later, when I was fourteen and my mother was pregnant with my brother, Giacomo, she told me that a rich old lady in town, Mrs. Bagnoli, remembered my Communion dress and wanted to buy it. My mother explained that with the money we could buy a stove to heat the kitchen.

It was worth it. With our first stove, we could burn wood, cook on top of it, and always have some hot water handy. Over time, we moved on to other stoves. My sister-in-law Clara gave that first stove it to an old lady who lived in the mountains. Now, many years later, it is still there, still turning out great meals.

Dough
1 ²/₃ cups all-purpose flour
1 ¹/₂ teaspoons baking powder
pinch salt
²/₃ cup sugar
1 stick (4 ounces) butter, softened
1 egg plus 2 egg yolks
1 teaspoon lemon zest

Filling
¹/₃ cup all-purpose flour
1 egg plus 2 egg yolks
1 teaspoon vanilla
³/₄ cup milk
¹/₂ cup sugar
1 teaspoon lemon zest
1 pound ricotta cheese (fresh, if possible)

Topping
1 egg yolk, lightly beaten
³/₄ cup pine nuts

FOR THE DOUGH:
Combine the flour, baking powder, and salt. Set aside.

In a food processor, combine the sugar, butter, egg, egg yolks, and lemon zest. Pulse until well combined. Slowly pulse in the flour mixture. Transfer the dough to an air-tight container, and chill in the refrigerator for at least 1 hour.

Preheat the oven to 300°F. Grease an 8-inch soufflé dish and set aside.

Remove half of the dough, and roll it out into a 10- or 11-inch round. Carefully transfer the dough to the prepared pan, and pat it into place in the bottom and up the sides of the pan. Return the remaining dough to the refrigerator until you are ready to use it. Bake the dough for 15 minutes. Remove from the oven, and let cool for 5 to 10 minutes.

Increase the oven temperature to 375°F.

FOR THE FILLING:
In a medium bowl, whisk together the flour, egg, egg yolks, and vanilla. Set aside.

Put the milk, sugar, and lemon zest in a small saucepan, and bring to a boil over medium heat. Remove it from the heat and slowly whisk it into the flour mixture, until thoroughly combined. Add the ricotta, and mix well. Pour the filling into the baked bottom crust.

Roll out the remaining dough into a 9-inch round. Carefully place this dough circle on top of the filling, and gently press its edges down the inside of the pan to connect it, where possible, to the lower crust.

FOR THE TOPPING:
Carefully brush the egg yolk on the top layer of dough. Pour the pine nuts on top and press them very gently into the dough.

Bake at 375°F for 15 minutes. Then reduce the temperature to 350°F, and bake for 30 minutes more, until the cake is a deep golden brown on top and the middle does not jiggle when the pan is tapped. Remove from the oven and let sit for at least 15 minutes before serving.

Serves 8.

Semifreddo Aurum *(Aurum Custard)*

AFTER OUR BAKERY SHUT DOWN and the extended family in Montecatini went their separate ways, my Aunt Livia got a job at the Casino Valadier, perhaps the most fashionable restaurant in Rome, and I would visit her. Many celebrities went there. When Livia knew there was someone famous coming she would bring me to the casino and put me on the roof. From there, I could see the people at the elegant parties on the terrazzo. I saw the wedding of Tyrone Power and Linda Christian, which was just about all the glamour my young heart could stand. Orson Welles and Rita Hayworth were frequent diners. I always associate my memories of the Casino Valadier with the semifreddo that they made with liqueur.

$^2/_3$ cup milk
2 tablespoons Aurum liqueur or
   3 tablespoons Grand Marnier
1 teaspoon orange zest
6 egg yolks

$^2/_3$ cup sugar
$^1/_8$ teaspoon unflavored gelatin
1 cup heavy cream, whipped
sliced fresh fruit, for serving

Combine the milk, liqueur, and orange zest in a small saucepan. Bring to a boil over medium heat Remove from the heat, and let cool for 5 minutes.

Whisk together the egg yolks and sugar. Slowly add it to the cooled egg mixture, whisking well. Add the gelatin, and let cool for 10 minutes more. Gently stir in the whipped heavy cream, just until it is well combined.

Transfer the mixture to an airtight rectangular container, and freeze for at least 3 hours or overnight. Slice, and serve immediately with fresh fruit.

Serves 4.

Torta della Nonna

THIS IS ANOTHER DESSERT from my mother. We call it Torta Della Nonna because Giovanna is my children's nonna, and I learned it when she would cook for my boys. She got the recipe from her cousin. I also learned a variation of it from Piero, who is married to Sirio's sister, Clara, and is a fine baker in Montecatini. I gave Piero's recipe to the pastry chefs at Circo and they changed it a little here and there and the result is even better. It takes a lot to get my boys to admit you could possibly make improvements on their grandma's recipe.

Filling

1 quart milk
⅔ cup granulated sugar
½ cup all-purpose flour
1 egg, lightly beaten
½ teaspoon vanilla extract

Pastry

1 ⅔ cups all-purpose flour
1 stick (4 ounces) plus 3 tablespoons softened butter
⅔ cup granulated sugar
2 whole eggs
2 egg yolks, separated
grated zest of 1 lemon
½ cup pine nuts
¼ cup confectioners' sugar

FOR THE FILLING:
In a medium saucepan, bring the milk to a boil over medium-high heat. Add the sugar and flour and mix well. Add the egg, mixing it in very quickly. Return the mixture to a boil. Reduce the heat and simmer until the mixture begins to thicken enough so that it coats the back of a wooden spoon. Remove from the heat and let cool for 10 minutes. Stir in the vanilla. Set aside.

FOR THE PASTRY:
Using an electric mixer, combine the flour, butter, and sugar, and mix well. Add the whole eggs, one at a time, mixing well after each addition. Add 1 of the egg yolks and the lemon zest and mix well. Cover and refrigerate for 2 hours.

Preheat the oven to 400° F. Grease a 13-inch round cake pan. Divide the dough in half. Place half the dough in the prepared pan and, using lightly floured fingers, spread it to cover the bottom of the pan. Pour in the filling.

Roll out the remaining pastry dough into a 13-inch round and gently place it on top of the filling. Puncture the top with a fork in a few places. Lightly beat the remaining egg yolk and carefully brush it on the pastry. Sprinkle the pine nuts on top.

Bake the torte in the preheated oven for 45 minutes. Decrease the temperature to 350° F and bake for 15 minutes, until the pastry is deep golden brown. Remove from the oven and let sit for 15 minutes. Dust with confectioners' sugar and serve warm.

Serves 8.

Ciambella Coffee Cake

WHEN I MOVED TO AMERICA, my best friend, Paola, came for a visit at the same time that my father was staying with us. Paola was reminiscing about our younger days and remembered the cake that my father used to make for birthdays and holidays. As she talked, she got hungrier until finally she asked my father if he would make a ciambella for us. Of course he said yes. He baked it then left it to cool on the windowsill. Then my son, Mauro, who was just a baby, pushed it out the window. When we peered out the window the next morning, there was Papa's cake in a big puddle. It had absorbed a lot of water and swollen to three times its normal size. Poor Paola was disappointed but quickly got over it when my dad whipped up another one.

Cake

4 cups all-purpose flour

1 ½ cups sugar

1 stick (4 ounces) plus 1 tablespoon softened butter

4 whole eggs

2 egg yolks, separated

⅓ cup milk

2 teaspoons baking soda

Preheat the oven to 400° F. Grease a small soufflé cup and a 20-inch nonstick round pizza pan or a large non-stick baking sheet. Place the soufflé cup upside-down in the center of the pizza pan or baking sheet. Set aside.

Using an electric mixer, combine the flour, 1 ¼ cups sugar, butter, whole eggs, 1 egg yolk, milk, and baking soda. Mix well.

In a small bowl, stir together the remaining egg yolk and ¼ cup sugar, until you have a crumbly paste, adding more sugar if necessary to achieve this texture.

Spoon the cake batter onto the prepared pan, making a ring around the inverted soufflé pan. Sprinkle the crumbly mixture on top.

Bake in the preheated oven for 15 minutes. Reduce the heat to 350° F, and bake for 15 minutes more, until the cake is a deep golden color and a cake tester inserted in the center comes out clean. Let cool for at least 10 minutes, then remove the inverted soufflé pan. Serve warm or cooled.

Serves 10.

sirio's favorites

Sirio's Favorites

WHEN I WAS A YOUNG TEENAGER, I had to grow up very quickly to adjust to a few big changes in our life. My dad, who was equally renowned for his baking as his bocci-playing, was not so good at picking horses. To make ends meet my mother took in a lot of sewing work and I helped her. I had to leave school so that I could look after my infant brother while my mother worked. I prepared most of the family food and it was in those years that I became an accomplished home cook.

After I put the baby to bed and cleaned up from dinner, my mother and I would work on her dressmaking and sometimes we would sing to pass the time. I always loved to sing and dance. My mother made me the official fabric steamer (she taught me that if you steam the fabric before you cut it, there will be no shrinkage).

After a few years, I became friendly with one of the local girls, Clara Maccioni. That was how I met this fabulous young dancer, her brother, Sirio. To hear him tell the story, we met earlier when I would go to family affairs with his sister but I think, "he had his eye on me before I had my eye on him," as we say.

My first memory of Siro is when I was nineteen or twenty. He was beginning his career. From a start as a busboy and waiter in Montecatini he traveled the world: Germany, France, the Caribbean, America. I was starting to be interested

in boys (the idea of boys, not any one boy), when Sirio came back from Cuba with a bunch of cha-cha and mambo records—the newest stuff like Don Marino Barreto, the inventor of cha cha. All the girls stood in line to dance with Sirio and I was one of them. We were good dancing partners and began to like each other, but I could tell it only from the dancing because Sirio wasn't the kind of guy to say "I love you, young lady."

One night there was a singing contest in a town nearby. "You have a beautiful voice," Sirio said. "Go ahead and sing in the contest." So Sirio drove my mother and me to this amateur festival and to my surprise, I won the prize!"

The maestro of the band, Mauro Casini came up after the contest and asked if I would like to sing in his band.

"If you pay me," I said.

"I will," he answered, "but you have to take singing lessons twice a week."

I worked hard at becoming a singer in the relaxed jazzy style of Rosemary Clooney. Casini paid me well and I began to sing all over northern Italy. I didn't like the traveling part much—I missed my family, and in the

summertime, I missed seeing Sirio, who came back to Montecatini every year to visit.

The turning point came when I was offered a big recording contract if I moved to Rome. I had no intention of leaving my family and, to tell you the truth, I loved singing but I was not super-ambitious about it.

As the English say, "I had set my cap" on Sirio, who was living in America.

"It may be a long time," he said, "before I can bring you over."

"That's okay, I can wait," I told him.

And I did. We have been married now for thirty-eight years, with three sons, three grand-children, and two giant dogs that belong to Marco and I end up minding them whenever he travels.

Panzanella (Bread Salad)

MY FATHER wasn't always very strict with us, but he did have one commandment nobody dared to break: "Never throw away old bread!" Since he was a baker, you would think he might have wanted people to throw away old bread so that they had to buy fresh bread. But he had pride in his product and couldn't stand to see it tossed out after all the work that went into it. In the summer, when cucumbers, tomatoes, and onions are all at their peak of flavor and everyone has a little garden—this is one of the easiest, and quickest recipes and it doesn't heat up the kitchen.

4 thick slices day-old Tuscan bread or any peasant-style
   bread
2 large tomatoes, coarsely chopped
1 medium red onion, coarsely chopped
1 medium cucumber, peeled and coarsely chopped
1 small bunch basil, coarsely chopped (about ⅓ cup)

1 large clove garlic, coarsely chopped
extra-virgin olive oil
red wine vinegar
salt
black pepper
crushed red pepper

Soak the bread in water for 20 minutes to 2 hours (depending on how dry the bread is), until it is soft but not disintegrated. Remove the bread from the water and squeeze out as much water as you can. Discard the water. Coarsely chop the bread into ½-inch pieces. Toss with tomatoes, onion, cucumber, basil, and garlic. Dress well with oil, vinegar, salt, black pepper, and crushed red pepper to taste.

NOTE: The proportions and amounts of the dressing ingredients are flexible and up to your individual taste. You can try these amounts as a point of departure: ¼ cup oil, 1 tablespoon vinegar, ½ teaspoon salt, ½ teaspoon black pepper, and a pinch of crushed red pepper.

Serves 6.

The preparation of most Tuscan dishes is simple: usually salt, pepper and a little bit of garlic. I think this simplicity explains why you can eat a good amount of Tuscan food and feel good. It doesn't rely on heavy sauces or fat for flavor, just the ingredients. Even though I eat a lot when I go home every summer, I still lose weight. Give me perfect, fresh radicchio from the garden and I am satisfied.

Cinzia's Olives

On my most recent visit to Montecatini, my sister-in-law, Cinzia, requested some olives from the only olive tree in my garden. She cured them with this recipe and I served them to Sirio at dinner. "These are the best olives in the world!" he declared. It takes a long time for the olives to cure, but I swear it is worth the wait.

1 pound fresh black olives
6 tablespoons coarse salt
4 cloves garlic, thinly sliced

1 tablespoon orange zest
¼ cup olive oil

Wash and drain the olives. Spread the olives on a clean kitchen towel to dry thoroughly. When the olives are completely dry, divide them into four small jars. Put 1 tablespoon of the salt into each jar. Seal the jars, and shake well.

Shake each jar, and drain off any accumulated juice every day for 3 weeks. At the end of this period, remove the olives from the jars and towel dry. Divide them again into four small jars. Set aside.

Combine the remaining 2 tablespoons salt with the garlic and orange zest. Divide this mixture among the four jars filled with olives. Seal the jars and shake well. Shake each jar, and drain off any accumulated juice every few days for 10 more days. Combine the olives with the olive oil. They are now ready to eat, or they can be stored for 4 months in the refrigerator or 2 months at room temperature.

Makes about 1 pound cured olives.

Riso con Fagioli *(Rice and Bean Soup)*

IN TUSCANY we learned to love beans. We had to, because in the old days meat was never very easy to come by. Everyone makes a rice and bean soup, so I don't remember exactly where I got this recipe. It's probably a mix of all the aunts and mothers and grandmothers of Tuscany. It is a thick, hearty soup, full of onions and beans and it is very economical.

$1/2$ pound dried cannellini (Great Northern) beans (about $1 1/2$ cups)

salt

$1/2$ cup olive oil, plus more for drizzling

1 large red onion

4 cloves garlic

2 leaves fresh rosemary

1 thin slice prosciutto, torn into small pieces

$1/4$ cup tomato paste

2 quarts hot water

$1 1/2$ cups rice

pepper

Place the beans in a large saucepan with plenty of water to cover. Season with salt to taste, and 2 tablespoons of the olive oil. Cook until the beans are soft, 45 to 60 minutes. Strain and set aside.

Chop the onion, garlic, rosemary, and prosciutto in a food processor, pulsing until well chopped but not pureed. In a large saucepan, heat the remaining 6 tablespoons olive oil over medium heat for 2 to 3 minutes. Add the tomato paste and cook 1 minute more. Add the hot water and cook for 30 minutes. Pass this mixture through a food mill along with the beans.

Return the puree to the saucepan. Add the rice and bring to a boil. Cover, reduce, and simmer, until the rice is cooked, about 20 minutes. Serve hot with a little drizzle of olive oil.

Serves 4.

Peperonata

MY MOTHER, GIOVANNA, taught me how to make this. Sirio loves it and would have it every day if he could. It's kind of a Tuscan ratatouille although we don't always use eggplant in it the way the French do. The real stars are the peppers. A good fifty percent of the recipe must be peppers. The finished vegetable stew is a wonderful side dish that goes with many things: bollito, steak, grilled fish, a simple risotto. The odds are if it comes out of a Tuscan kitchen, you can serve pepperonata with it.

1 clove garlic, minced

2 green bell peppers, cored, seeded, and cut into $^1/_2$-inch strips

1 yellow bell pepper, cored, seeded, and cut into $^1/_2$-inch strips

1 red bell pepper, cored, seeded, and cut into $^1/_2$-inch strips

4 carrots, peeled and sliced

2 large white onions, peeled and coarsely chopped

2 tablespoons coarsely chopped fresh parsley

$^1/_2$ large eggplant, coarsely chopped

4 small zucchini, coarsely chopped

2 tomatoes, coarsely chopped

1 stalk celery, finely chopped

1 clove garlic, minced

3 basil leaves, coarsely chopped

pinched dried oregano

crushed red pepper to taste

$^1/_4$ cup olive oil

1 tablespoon balsamic vinegar

Put all ingredients into a large saucepan or ovenproof baking dish. Cook over medium heat on the stovetop or at 350° F in the oven for 1 hour, stirring occasionally, until all the ingredients are very soft. Add a little water if necessary to keep the vegetables moist.

Serves 4.

Farinata di Cavolo Nero *(Cornmeal with Black Cabbage)*

SIRIO'S NONNA ASSUNTA made this. In our region cavolo nero, or black cabbage, is always grown in the family's garden. These days, I see it in some of the more ambitious supermarkets. This hearty dish acquires a delicious smoky aroma when it is made the old-fashioned way, in a big iron pot over a fire, cooked slowly. In New York we get our cavolo nero from Ed Jobbi, a farmer who raises special vegetables a little north of the city. I used to make this dish for Craig Claiborne, the former restaurant critic for the *New York Times*. I was pretty nervous the first time he invited us to his house in the Hamptons. I cooked Pasta Primavera, Gnocchi ala Roma, Crostini Toscana, and Cavolo Nero. The whole time Craig was in the kitchen with his IBM typewriter, "dissecting" my cooking.

½ cup extra-virgin olive oil

1 black cabbage (Tuscan kale or cavolo nero), coarsely chopped

2 small stalks celery, coarsely chopped

2 tablespoons coarsely chopped fresh parsley

1 quart hot water

1 cup cornmeal

salt

pepper

extra-virgin olive oil, for drizzling

In a medium saucepan, heat the olive oil over medium-high heat. Add the cabbage and celery and cook for 3 to 5 minutes. Add the parsley and cook for 1 minute. Add the hot water and cook for 20 minutes or more, until the cabbage is very soft and thoroughly cooked.

Bring to a vigorous boil. Add the cornmeal, a bit at a time, stirring constantly and maintaining the boil. Season with salt and pepper to taste. Reduce the heat and cook, stirring occasionally, for a total of 20 minutes from the time you started adding the cornmeal. Serve in bowls with olive oil drizzled on top.

NOTE: The black cabbage can be difficult to find. You can substitute Savoy cabbage in this recipe.

Serves 4.

My Three Sons: Marco

Most of the cooking my mom did was to please my father. There was some Fred Flintstone in my dad: very boisterous. But Wilma was the love of his life, much as my mom is my dad's. Speaking of TV, Mom learned a lot of her English by watching I Love Lucy. Our life was a little like theirs: Ricky Ricardo was off to the nightclub (my dad at Le Cirque) while Mom (Lucy) ran the home. My brothers and I couldn't have asked for a better playmate.

Little White Onions Sauteed with Balsamic Vinegar

SIRIO ALWAYS TELLS modern gourmets that we didn't have balsamic vinegar in the old days. For most of us that was true. The real balsamico from Modena is aged for many years and is very expensive. This recipe was often made with regular vinegar and a little sugar. Nowadays I often have balsamico and I use it with small onions. Per my husband's request I make it for just about every special occasion meal.

2 pounds small white onions, peeled

1/2 cup olive oil

1 tablespoon balsamic vinegar

salt

pepper

Place onions, olive oil, and vinegar in a heavy saucepan on medium heat. Stir to coat onions well. Cover and cook about 45 minutes, stirring occasionally, until the onions are thoroughly cooked. Add salt and pepper to taste. Serve warm.

Serves 4.

Tonno e Fagioli *(Tuna and Beans)*

I FIND that the most delicious tuna is a high-quality import from Portugal or Italy. For the beans, you can used dried or fresh cannelli. In Tuscany we have a very special bean, the sorana. It grows only in a little village near Lucca on a few plots of land. Even natives have a hard time getting the prized beans. They are beautiful, delicate, and so soft that you don't even need to peel them. Truly there is nothing like the sorana bean. Still, this is a great recipe—a simple salad with regular white beans.

½ pound dried cannellini (Great Northern) beans
   (about 1 ½ cups)
2 cups hot water
1 clove garlic
3 fresh sage leaves or 1 teaspoon dried sage

six 6-ounce cans tuna
1 medium red onion, peeled and very thinly sliced
½ cup olive oil
salt
pepper

In a large saucepan, combine the dried beans and hot water and bring to a boil. Boil for 2 minutes. Cover and let sit for 1 hour. Drain the beans and return to the pot.

Add the garlic clove and sage leaves to the beans. Cover with water and bring to boil. Boil just until the beans are tender, 10 to 15 minutes. Drain. Discard the garlic and sage. Transfer the beans to a large bowl.

Drain the tuna and add it to the beans along with the onion. Mix well. Season with the olive oil and salt and pepper to taste. Serve immediately (or refrigerate for up to a few days before serving).

Serves 8.

My Three Sons: Mauro

We always have a political argument about food in Italy. Is the food right-wing or left-wing? Nobody in America ever asks if apple pie is a Democrat or Republican, but in Italy we contemplate these things. The focus in Tuscany is definitely more on the common people's food. Today you go to a top restaurant in Florence and the cuisine is less based on the aristocracy of the Medicis and more on the ribollita, pappa pomodoro, and panzanella of the peasants. When my American friends ask my dad where they should go for an awesome meal in Tuscany, I am sure they are thinking about white truffles and Chianina steak. Boy, are they surprised when they follow his directions to a little place in the marshes of Padule, near where he grew up, where all they serve is tripe, chicken liver, frog stew, fried eels . . . the real food of the Tuscan marshes.

Dentice alla Livornese *(Red Snapper, Livorno Style)*

SIRIO LOVES THE LIVORNESE STYLE, with wine and tomatoes. Maybe it has something to do with the fact that Livorno has a very down-to-earth tradition, not like some of the chi-chi seaside towns of Verisiglia, closer to Montecatini. Whenever I had a hard time selling the kids on baccalà, they would usually snap up this red snapper.

2 pounds red snapper, cleaned and deboned
1/4 cup all-purpose flour
3 tablespoons olive oil
1/3 cup finely chopped flat-leaf parsley
1 clove garlic, finely chopped

1 1/2 cups peeled and crushed canned tomatoes
1/4 cup white wine
salt
pepper

Cut the snapper into large pieces. Thoroughly coat the pieces in the flour.

Heat the olive oil in a large skillet. Gently fry the snapper pieces over medium heat, just until they begin to turn golden but not entirely cooked 3 to 5 minutes per side. Remove the fish from the pan and set aside.

Add the parsley and garlic to the skillet. Increase heat to medium-high, and cook for 2 minutes. Add the tomatoes and wine and simmer for 10 minutes. Season with salt and pepper to taste.

Return the fish to the pan and cover. Reduce the heat and simmer for 10 minutes without disturbing the fish.

Carefully transfer the fish pieces to warmed plates and cover with the tomato sauce from the pan. Serve immediately.

Serves 4.

Baccalà Livornese *(Salt Cod, Livorno Style)*

AFTER WE WERE MARRIED we lived in a sixth-floor walkup. On the ground floor was Lutece, one of the top restaurants in New York. Andre Soltner, who was the owner and chef, is still one of our closest friends. We were part of a little community of chefs and food lovers: Andre, Pierre Franey (another great chef and cookbook author), Craig Claiborne, William Zeckendorf—too many to remember. And almost too many for our apartment. Our place was tiny. Sirio bought twelve folding chairs and a folding table. It was a tight squeeze. One day Sirio said, "Make some baccalà, everybody will love it." Everybody in Italy loves this salted dried cod. Many important people would trudge up the stairs for my baccalà. I remember Mr. Levitt, one of the biggest real-estate developers in America, was wild about it and would come anytime Sirio mentioned it.

I pound dried cod

¼ cup all-purpose flour

I cup olive oil

I red onion, coarsely chopped

½ cup finely chopped parsley

3 cloves garlic, finely chopped

I cup peeled and crushed
   canned tomatoes

crushed red pepper

I cup water

¼ cup dry white wine

boiled potatoes, for serving

Soak cod in water overnight. Drain and dry in a cloth or paper towels.

Dip the cod in the flour to lightly coat.

Heat the olive oil in a large saucepan over medium-high heat. Fry the cod fish for about 3 minutes per side, until light golden brown. Remove the fish from the oil and set aside.

Pour off half of the oil from the pan. Return the pan with the remaining oil to medium-high heat. Add the onions and cook for 2 to 3 minutes, until they begin to soften. Add the parsley and garlic, and cook for I minute. Add the tomatoes, wine, water, and crushed red pepper. Simmer for 15 minutes. Add the codfish, cover, and simmer 10 minutes longer. Serve hot with boiled potatoes.

Serves 4.

SIRIO SPEAKS

My grandmother, Assunta, made baccalà all the time on the farm. She would show me all the herbs, the cardoons, the wild asparagus. We would get eggs from the hens and pick some wild onions then go back to the kitchen where I helped her make frittata. We had grapes that made very good wine, or at least we all thought it was very good. The thing I remember the most was our fig tree. It grew right outside my window. I loved it so much. Now when I travel all over the world and see so much hustle and bustle, thinking of that fig tree brings me back to what normal life is supposed to be.

Calamaretti con Piselli *(Baby Calamari with Peas)*

NONNA LEONELLA used to make this for me, a colorful mix of tender baby calamari, with wine, tomatoes, parsley, garlic, and peas. Oddly I never prepared it in Italy. But when Sirio and I made our home in New York it was one of the tastes of our common childhood that we both loved to return to.

½ cup olive oil

1 ¼ pounds squid (the smaller, the better), cleaned and sliced into rings

¼ cup finely chopped parsley

2 cloves garlic

1 pound frozen peas

1 cup water

1 cup peeled canned tomatoes, coarsely chopped

½ cup white wine

salt

black pepper or crushed red pepper

In a large skillet, heat the oil over medium-high heat. Add the squid, and cook for 5 minutes, stirring occasionally. Add the parsley and garlic, and cook for 2 minutes. Add the peas, tomatoes, water, and wine, and mix well. Season with salt and pepper to taste. Reduce heat to low, cover, and cook for 40 minutes longer, stirring occasionally. Serve hot.

Serves 4.

Piccone alla Contadina *(Squab, Peasant Style)*

THOUGH THIS RECIPE is from Sirio's great-uncle, Guido, it is similar to the one we made in my family. Uncle Guido was a chef at the Croce di Malta, one of the better hotels in Montecatini. One of the first times I cooked for Sirio's family out at their farmhouse, Guido was there.

Sirio's sister, Clara, and I made a very simple Tuscan toast for an appetizer: butter spread with anchovies. Guido came over, took one look and said, "I don't like how you are doing this. Let me show you my way." For a moment I was worried—I thought Uncle Guido didn't like me. Running anxiously up and down the stairs, I even twisted my ankle. The dinner was a success, though, and I thank Uncle Guido for all his recipes.

8 to 10 dried black mushrooms, preferably Italian
4 squabs (pigeon), halved, livers reserved
salt
pepper
1/2 cup olive oil, divided
1 clove garlic, thinly sliced
onion, finely chopped (1 cup)

1 teaspoon dried rosemary or 6 small fresh rosemary
  leaves
1/2 cup dry red wine
2 cups crushed fresh or canned tomatoes
fresh white mushrooms, thinly sliced (1 cup)
1/4 cup tomato paste diluted in 1/3 cup water
polenta (see recipe, page 41), for serving

Soak the dried mushrooms in cold water for 30 minutes or more. Generously coat the squab with salt and pepper. Set aside.

Heat 3/8 cup of the olive oil in a large heavy skillet over high heat. Add the garlic and cook, stirring, for 30 seconds. Add the squab cut side down and brown for 3 minutes. Turn the squab over and brown for 3 minutes more. Add the onion, rosemary, wine, tomatoes, and salt and pepper to taste.

Drain the black mushrooms, and squeeze out as much water as you can; discard the water. Add the mushrooms to the squab. Keep on low heat.

In another skillet, heat the remaining 2 tablespoons olive oil over medium-high heat. Add the fresh mushrooms, and cook until they begin to wilt, about 5 minutes. Add these mushrooms to the squab. Cook for 5 minutes more.

Add the diluted tomato paste to the squab. Cover, and cook for 30 minutes, stirring and turning the squab occasionally. Add the squab livers, and cook for 30 minutes longer. Serve immediately with hot polenta.

Serves 4.

Zucchini Ripieni (*Stuffed Zucchini*)

ANOTHER ONE of Nonna Leonella's Tuscan specialties. It is an ingenious way to use leftover veal or beef, especially with a little mortadella. The mortadella, a Bolognese cold cut, is my addition. I prefer it to our Tuscan prosciutto in this recipe. Mortadella has such a stupendous flavor. Although it is sometimes compared to American bologna, a true Bolognese would never make the comparison.

6 medium zucchini (1 $\frac{1}{2}$ to 2 pounds)

$\frac{1}{2}$ breast of chicken, cooked (about $\frac{1}{2}$ pound)

2 thick slices mortadella (about $\frac{1}{4}$ pound)

$\frac{1}{4}$ cup ricotta cheese

$\frac{1}{4}$ cup Parmesan cheese

1 egg, lightly beaten

1 small bunch flat-leaf parsley, finely chopped (about $\frac{1}{3}$ cup)

$\frac{1}{2}$ clove garlic, finely chopped

1 to 2 pinches freshly grated nutmeg

salt

pepper

bread crumbs

1 small stalk celery, very finely chopped

1 small carrot, peeled and very finely chopped

1 small onion, peeled and very finely chopped

2 canned peeled tomatoes

$\frac{1}{4}$ cup olive oil

Preheat the oven to 350° F. Grease a large baking pan. Set aside.

Cut the zucchini in half lengthwise and then in half crosswise again (see note below). Scrape out about half of the white center, leaving the dark skin intact. Discard the scrapings. Set aside the hollowed out skins.

In a food processor, mix the chicken, mortadella, ricotta, Parmesan, egg, parsley, garlic, nutmeg, and salt and pepper to taste. Stuff the meat mixture into the zucchini. Pat bread crumbs on the ends of each of the stuffed zucchini. Arrange the zucchini skin sides down in the prepared pan. Sprinkle the celery, carrot, and onion pieces over the zucchini. Crush the tomatoes in your hand, drizzling the tomato juices and pieces onto the zucchini. Sprinkle with the olive oil. Cover with aluminum foil and bake for 45 minutes. Remove the foil and bake for 15 minutes longer.

NOTE: Sirio prefers his stuffed zucchini as described above, but I prefer them cored. To make everyone happy, I usually make them both ways. To core: remove ends, cut in half through the middle, and carefully scoop out the inside with a table knife, leaving the skin intact.

Serves 4.

My Three Sons: Mauro

Italians are very respectful of food. If there's a little bit left over, they'll save it and use it the next day. I remember going to visit my Aunt Clara or my grandmother. The meals usually consisted of mangiarini, "little morsels" that featured leftovers. "Oh," Clara would say, "I had a few zucchini left and some chicken and veal, so I made a little stuffed zucchini." Our meals were always made up of these little things, always a surprise because they were made according to whatever was left over.

Spezzatino (Veal Stew)

One day my brothers and I were at a Jets game. When we came home it was like Defcon Four in the house because one of our dearest friends, Mr. Zeckendorf, was coming for dinner. Mom was a whirlwind of last-minute preparations and my dad, I have to confess, looked a little grumpy. It turned out that the night before he had gone into the family's private wine stash and had put aside a bottle of Romanee Conti to go with the spezzatino. The next day my mom was cooking and she saw this dusty old bottle in the kitchen. She opened it, took a swig and it tasted so good she decided to use it for the spezzatino! My dad was pretty worked up over this, which was understandable but mom laid down the law. "If you don't simmer down, I am going on strike and Mr. Zeckendorf doesn't eat tonight." Dad had no choice but to calm down and find another bottle of wine to go with what turned out to be the most expensive spezzatino in history.
—MARCO

1 pound veal stew meat, cut into cubes
1 tablespoon all-purpose flour
1 tablespoon olive oil
1 large red onion, cut into small wedges
1 whole clove garlic
1 sprig fresh rosemary, or 1 teaspoon dried
1/2 cup white wine

1 1/2 cups canned peeled tomatoes
1 cup water
2 medium carrots, peeled and cut crosswise
    into 1/2-inch thick slices
1 tablespoon tomato paste
salt
pepper

In a medium bowl, toss the veal cubes with the flour until the veal is well coated. Heat the oil in a large skillet over medium-high heat. Add the veal, and cook until it begins to brown, about 5 minutes. Add the onion, garlic, and rosemary, and cook for about 2 minutes more, just until the onion begins to soften. Add the white wine, and stir to deglaze the pan, about 2 minutes. Add the tomatoes, 1/2 cup water, carrots, and tomato paste.

Cover and reduce the heat to the lowest setting. Cook the stew for 1 to 1 1/2 hours, checking and stirring occasionally, until the meat is soft and fully cooked. Add additional water if needed to keep the stew from drying out. Serve warm.

Serves 4.

Pollo al Mattone (Brick-Pressed Chicken)

CRISPY JUICY CHICKEN is a universal favorite. In Tuscany we use real bricks to press the chicken down so that it cooks quickly and evenly. How did Tuscans get this idea? Just look around any Tuscan town; the long elegant Tuscan brick is everywhere. No doubt it was what they used to make the first pressed sandwiches, or panini. This chicken reminds me of when the Americans arrived in 1945. Food was still hard to come by. My Uncle Renato was working for the Americans.

My Holy Communion was coming up, so Renato kept an eye out for something to have for the celebration meal. One of the American soldiers offered two chickens on the condition that my uncle invite him and a buddy for dinner. Who could blame him for preferring a home-cooked Italian meal over army rations? Renato accepted the chickens, brought the soldiers home with him and we all celebrated my Communion.

1 young chicken (3 to 4 pounds)
juice of 1 lemon
salt
pepper
olive oil

Rinse the chicken and pat dry with paper towels. Pour the lemon juice over the chicken, and spread it with your hands to coat the entire bird, inside and out. Lightly salt and pepper the entire chicken. Cover and refrigerate for 1 to 2 hours.

Discard the backbone of the chicken. Pound the chicken with a meat pounder so that it lies flat.

Heat a large heavy skillet and two clean bricks over medium-high until very hot. Coat the chicken on both sides with olive oil. Put the chicken in the skillet in one layer, and place the bricks on top. Reduce the heat to medium and cook the chicken for 10 minutes. Remove the bricks, turn the children over, and replace the bricks. Repeat the turning process every 10 to 15 minutes. Cook for 30 to 40 minutes total, until the chicken is no longer pink, juices run clear when the breast is pierced to the bone, and drumsticks move easily. The bird will be crisp and golden on the outside, and juicy on the inside.

NOTE: If you are uncertain about the cleanliness of your bricks, then wrap them in aluminum foil before using. If you do not have access to any bricks, you can substitute a very heavy iron skillet or a large pan filled with water.

Serves 4.

We have had many well-known people come to visit us in Montecatini: Tony Bennett and Lee Iacocca among them, but no one stayed in the kitchen as much as Woody Allen did. He came to cook with Egi for three days. He was a good student. He especially liked fried things— crispy pollo a mattone, zucchini, and of course, like every American, he wanted lots of pasta. Just like a character in his movies he seemed anxious, always making sure there was no butter involved. He was so relieved to find that we always used olive oil.

Schiacciata con L'Uva *(Sweet Bread with Grapes)*

THIS RECIPE IS VERY, very old. Schiacciata is a traditional bread made during the wine harvest and I am told that it has been made since Etruscan times. Lorenzo de Medici, who was known more as a prince than a cook, supposedly had a recipe for it. It always tastes so right for the season. This has sweet raisins in it and my kids were never very big dried-fruit fans. I make it anyway for my husband and me.

1/4 cup olive oil, plus more for drizzling
Pizza Dough (see recipe, page 27)
1 pound ripe seedless red grapes, rinsed and dried well

3/4 cup sugar
pinch salt

Preheat the oven to 400°F. Grease a 9-by-9-inch baking pan. Knead the olive oil into the pizza dough. Divide the dough in half. Put one half of the dough in the prepared pan. Pat and press the dough with your fingers to cover the bottom of the pan. Spread the grapes on top of the dough evenly, and press them lightly into the dough. Sprinkle 1 to 2 tablespoons of the sugar over the grapes. Sprinkle on the salt. Cover with the remaining dough, pressing it lightly into the grapes below. Sprinkle the remaining sugar over the dough and drizzle with a little olive oil.

Bake the bread for 30 minutes, until deep golden brown. Remove from the oven and let rest for 15 minutes before serving.

Serves 8 to 12.

Sausage Stew with White Beans

WHEN SIRIO wants some real Italian cooking in the middle of a day at Le Cirque he walks two blocks over to Circo, our Italian restaurant on Fifty-fifth Street that I run with my sons. Quite often he asks for sausage stew. It is one of the recipes that his grandmother made for him. Sometimes when we have friends over and Sirio wants to show off my cooking, he requests sausage and beans. And even if he is showing off, I know he is genuinely hungry for some, too.

$\frac{1}{2}$ pound dried cannellini (Great Northern) beans (about 1 $\frac{1}{2}$ cups)

2 cups hot water

2 leaves fresh sage

1 clove garlic plus 2 cloves garlic, finely chopped

$\frac{1}{2}$ cup plus 2 tablespoons olive oil

8 Italian sausages

1 large red onion, peeled and coarsely chopped

1 bay leaf

2 tablespoons white wine

2 cups canned crushed tomatoes

salt

pepper

2 cups polenta (see recipe, page 41)

In a large saucepan, combine the dried beans and hot water and bring to a boil. Boil for 2 minutes. Cover and let sit for 1 hour. Drain the beans and return to the pot.

Add the sage, whole garlic clove, and 1 tablespoon of the olive oil to the large saucepan. Cover with water and bring to a boil. Boil just until the beans are tender, 10 to 15 minutes. Drain. Discard the garlic and save. Set the beans aside.

Puncture the sausages with a fork so that they will release their fat as they cook.

In a large pot, cook the sausages with 1 tablespoon of the olive oil over high heat until browned. Set the sausages aside. Discard the juices from the pan. Reduce the heat to medium-high. Add the onion, bay leaf, and remaining $\frac{1}{2}$ cup of olive oil and cook just until the onion begins to soften. Add the chopped garlic and cook for 2 minutes. Add the wine and cook for another 2 minutes. Reduce the head to medium-low, add the tomatoes, and return the sausages to the pot.

Cover the pot and cook for about 30 minutes, checking and stirring often to prevent sticking. If the stew becomes too dry or begins to stick, add $\frac{1}{4}$ cup water. When the stew is almost ready, add the reserved beans and cook for 5 minutes. Season with salt and pepper to taste.

Serve the stew with a large spoonful of polenta.

NOTE: The stew can also be made without the beans.

Serves 4.

SIRIO SPEAKS

My grandfather and my uncle were traditional butchers, which means that when it came time for neighboring farmers to kill a pig, they were asked to perform the operation. The pig-killing was almost a festival. Friends and family helped prepare food from every part of the pig. Everything would disappear. We even saved the skin and used it for soup in the winter. I love pork loin slowly cooked with herbs and lard— kind of a confit. For dinner on the night of the killing we made frittelle with liver. The after-dinner activity would be roasting chestnuts and then my grandfather, Giuseppe, would recite from memory Dante's Divine Comedy, Machiavelli, or Bocaccio. With no radio around, this was the way of handing down culture and entertaining each other.

Mele al Forno *(Baked Apples)*

I KEEP MENTIONING how simple Tuscan food is and this recipe, more than any other, proves the point. It is nothing more than baked apple with some butter and cream in the core and sugar on top. Despite having grown accustomed to the fanciful caprices that our restaurants craft—spun sugar sculptures and fruit confits and impossibly thin puff pastries —my husband is of the opinion that there is no finer dessert than a baked apple, especially in the autumn.

4 Golden Delicious apples
$3/4$ cup sugar
4 tablespoons butter

2 tablespoons Grand Marnier
$1/2$ teaspoon vanilla extract

Preheat oven to 350° F. Thoroughly grease well a 9-by-9-inch baking pan. Set aside.

Cut the top $3/4$ inch off the apples, and set aside. Leaving the bottoms of the apples intact, scoop out the apple cores and discard.

Scoop out as much of the apple flesh as possible, leaving the skin intact, leaving enough flesh for the apples to remain standing upright (hollow to within $1/2$ to $3/4$ inch of the skin). Reserve the apple flesh.

Place the hollowed out apples and apple tops separately into the prepared pan. Sprinkle 1 tablespoon sugar inside each apple. Cover with aluminum foil, and bake for 40 minutes.

Chop up the apple flesh. Put it with the butter, remaining $1/2$ cup sugar, Grand Marnier, and vanilla in a small skillet. Cook over medium heat until the apple softens and the ingredients are well combined, 5 to 10 minutes. Set aside.

When the apple skins are cooked, remove from the oven, and stuff with the sautéed apples. Cover with the baked apple tops, and serve immediately.

Serves 4.

Poached Capon with Boiled Vegetables

ON OUR FIRST New Year's in New York I was pregnant and had terrible morning sickness, but still I felt I had to cook for the holiday. So I made this in our little walkup and Sirio invited our next-door neighbors—Mr. Bindi and his wife. Coincidentally, years before, Mr. Bindi had been the maitre d' at La Pace Hotel in Montecatini and helped Sirio get a job (his first) there.

Capon

3 quarts water
1 chicken bouillon cube
1 small capon (about 3 pounds)
1 small tomato, cut in half
1 large carrot, peeled
1 stalk celery
1 sprig basil
1 sprig parsley
1 teaspoon salt

Vegetables

3 small beets, peeled and halved
1 pound carrots, peeled and cut into 2-inch lengths
1 heart of a celery bunch, stalks separated
2 large white onions, peeled and
    quartered
1 fennel bulb, stalks cut into 6 to 8 pieces
3 potatoes, cleaned and halved

$^{1}/_{2}$ cup green sauce (see recipe, page 157)

FOR THE CAPON:
Bring the water to a boil with the bouillon cube in a very large stockpot. Add the capon to the pot and return to a boil. Reduce the heat, add the tomato, carrot, celery, parsley, basil, and salt, cover, and cook at the lowest simmer possible for 1 $^{1}/_{2}$ hours.

FOR THE VEGETABLES:
If possible, boil each of the vegetables separately for $^{1}/_{2}$ hour with water and salt to keep the flavors and colors distinct. Otherwise, boil the beets separately from the other vegetables. Cook the vegetables for 30 minutes until tender.

Remove the capon from the broth, and serve hot with the boiled vegetables and green sauce.

Serves 6.

SIRIO SPEAKS

Saturday on the farm we would do a bollito. Counting my grandparents and uncles and aunts and kids, we usually were about twelve people. In the morning we would kill a chicken and then Nonna Assunta would go to the butcher for meat bones and maybe breast of veal. The whole farmhouse would fill with a rich meaty aroma.

new york

A Tuscan Mother in New York

IN 1963, SIRIO AND I had been seeing one another for a while. He was working in New York at the Colony so the next step in our relationship was to see how I liked America. He arranged a tour for our band. I sang at Carnegie Hall, the Brooklyn Academy of Music and continued the tour in Philadelphia, Boston, Chicago, Toronto. I loved America. The next year I came back to America, Sirio got his citizenship and that July we were married. The following year Mario was born.

In the beginning our little apartment on Fiftieth Street was tight but fine. After Mario was born, though, the apartment was just too small. One of Sirio's customers at the Colony told him about a rent-controlled apartment on Sixty-second Street and we lived there until we finally had enough money to afford to

ONLY NEW YORK PERFORMANCE
— BY POPULAR DEMAND —
With the Songs of the "San Remo Festival '64"
SATURDAY, APRIL 11th at 8:30 P. M.
ERBERTO LANDI presents:
An Evening with Italy's romantic baritone
LUCIANO VIRGILI
(CAPITOL Records)
and all in person (from Italy)
THE DI MARA SISTERS   DINO GIACCA
PIA GABRIELI   EGIDIANA PALMIERI
FRANK BERNARDI Your Singing Emcee
Full Orchestra
Mr. Virgili's accompanist GASTONE DeAMBROGI
CARNEGIE HALL
57th Street and Seventh Avenue, N. Y. C.
Tickets (from $1.90 to $5.90) at Carnegie Hall Box Office (CI 7-7460)
or, for reservations, Landi Enterprises Inc. - 853 Seventh Ave., New York
19, N. Y. - Tel. JU 6-0588 - JU 6-0525.

OUR WEDDING

AFTER MY WEDDING, MARIO
TUCCI, THE OWNER OF DEL
MONICO'S, AT THE PIANO

IN THE SNOW OF
UPSTATE NEW YORK

OUTSIDE OF OUR FIRST APART-
MENT ON EAST FIFTIETH
STREET IN NEW YORK

Sirio and me with
Mario and Marco
in Montecatini

Mario and me
in Viareggio

buy our own place on Sixty-fourth Street. Although I gave up being a professional singer to be a full-time mother, I never regretted my decision even for one minute. I found that family was an easy choice. I loved watching my children sleeping, waking. I could look at them forever.

When the boys were young, I would take them to Central Park where they would play and we would picnic. Sirio joined us there on his day off. As the boys grew they played football and soccer. They even used to play tackle in the house, but that came to an end when Mauro broke a rib rough-housing with his brothers.

My sons were my little helpers in the kitchen, although sometimes the mess was more than the help was worth, but we enjoyed making pizza, singing, and stories about Italy. Every summer from June to August we went to Tuscany, so even though my sons are real American guys, I know they think of themselves as Tuscans too.

My three boys
and my mother
at the beach
in Pietiasanta

My three sons

Porcini Mushroom Crostini

ONE SUMMER Sirio was in New York and I had the kids with me in Montecatini. My brother Giacomo, Sirio's sister Clara, and his uncles Guido and Alberto joined us for a picnic in the woods on the hills above town. Alberto and Guido, who took pride in their abilities as mushroom hunters, used sticks to probe the ground and under leaves but they found nothing. Little Marco and I and were left alone, sitting on a blanket when all of a sudden Marco said, "Hey Mom, look!"

I was astonished. Just next to him was a mushroom that weighed more than a pound. He was so proud. The uncles made a big deal of it and that night little Marco polished off a man-size helping of mushroom crostinis.

½ cup olive oil

1 pound fresh porcini mushrooms, sliced

2 cloves garlic, minced

2 teaspoons tomato paste

¼ cup dry white wine

¼ cup water

salt

pepper

8 large, thick slices Tuscan bread, toasted

Heat the oil in a large, nonreactive skillet over medium-high heat. Add the mushrooms and garlic and cook, stirring frequently until they begin to brown, 10 to 12 minutes.

In a small bowl, dissolve the tomato paste in the white wine and water. Add the liquid to the mushrooms, and continue cooking until the liquids are absorbed, about 2 minutes. Season with salt and pepper to taste.

Serve the mushrooms warm on the toasted bread slices.

NOTE: If you cannot find fresh porcini mushrooms, you can use one pound of regular white mushrooms with 2 dried porcini mushrooms. Soak the dried porcinis as directed on their package. Strain and squeeze out the water that they soaked in. Finely chop the porcini mushrooms, and sauté them for 5 minutes before adding the regular mushrooms.

Serves 8.

Mushroom Soup

A wonderful cold-weather soup. When I was little, Nonna Augusta and I would pick mushrooms on the outskirts of town. In the fall the little mushrooms were very plentiful and we would fill our baskets with hundreds of them. She had her own secret for making sure the mushrooms wouldn't poison us: She would put a silver fork in the soup as it was cooking. "If the fork turns black," she would say, "we have to throw the soup away because we will all die. If the fork stays shiny we can eat the soup." The whole time that I stirred the soup I was terrified. Of course, don't take my Nonna's directions as the way to tell poisonous from safe mushrooms. Unless you are an expert, buy your mushrooms in a store. The soup will still be delicious.

$^1/_3$ cup olive oil

4 large porcini mushrooms (about $^1/_4$ pound), thinly sliced

1 medium white onion, finely chopped

1 tablespoon finely chopped fresh parsley

$^1/_8$ teaspoon dried nepitella or 1 sprig fresh (also called cat-mint)

4 cloves garlic, 2 finely chopped and 2 peeled and halved

1 quart chicken stock

1 small potato, peeled, boiled, and mashed with a fork

salt

pepper

4 slices Italian bread

olive oil, for drizzling

In a large saucepan, heat the olive oil over medium-high heat. Add the mushrooms and onions and cook until well wilted, 8 to 10 minutes. Add the parsley, nepitella, and chopped garlic, and cook for 1 minute. Add the chicken stock and potato and bring to a boil. Reduce the heat to medium and boil for 20 minutes. Season with salt and pepper to taste.

Lightly rub the halved garlic on the bread and drizzle with a little olive oil. Toast until golden brown. Place a slice of toasted bread in each bowl and pour the soup on top.

NOTE: If you cannot find fresh porcini mushrooms, you can use $^1/_4$ pound regular mushrooms with 2 dried porcini mushrooms. Soak the porcinis as directed on their package. Strain and squeeze out the water that they soaked in. Finely chop the porcini mushrooms, and sauté them for 5 minutes before adding the regular mushrooms.

NOTE: The herb nepitella is very difficult to find in the United States You can substitute $^1/_3$ basil, $^1/_3$ mint, and $^1/_3$ oregano. Thus, for this recipe, you would use a tiny pinch of each.

Serves 4.

Tortino di Porri (Leek Soufflé)

YOU WILL NOT FIND THIS RECIPE in a typical Tuscan cookbook because I made it up one day when the editors of a magazine came to my house for a photo shoot. Sirio and the kids love this dish, so it became part of the Maccionis' "typical Tuscan" home recipes. It features leeks, which are very nice vegetables but few recipes call for them as the star ingredient. Sirio likes them boiled, but I prefer them sautéed so that they caramelize and develop deeper flavor. As far as this dish goes, he agrees with me.

2 tablespoons olive oil

1/4 pound leeks (about 2), trimmed, well cleaned, and cut crosswise into 1-inch pieces

1 tablespoon all-purpose flour

3 eggs, lightly beaten

1/2 cup grated Parmesan cheese

1/2 cup heavy cream

1 teaspoon finely chopped parsley

1/4 teaspoon minced garlic

1/2 teaspoon salt

Preheat the oven to 325 F. Grease a small soufflé dish (about 5 inches). Place it in a larger baking dish filled with three-quarters inch hot water.

In a medium skillet, heat the olive oil over medium heat. Add the leeks and cook until soft and easily cut with a fork, but not browned, about 20 minutes. Remove from the heat.

Put the leeks in a medium bowl with the flour and combine well. Add the eggs, Parmesan, cream, parsley, garlic, and salt and gently combine. Pour the mixture into the prepared soufflé dish. Bake about 55 minutes, until the mixture is well set and the top begins to turn golden brown. Serve warm.

Serves 4.

Cauliflower Strascicato in Padella

THE OTHER NIGHT I was preparing dinner for Sirio and me and I made this quick and simple side dish featuring cauliflower and capers. My mother used to make it for us and Sirio has always liked it. "Why don't you put this in your book?" he said as he finished off a second helping. So here it is.

1 head cauliflower

¼ cup olive oil

4 cloves garlic, minced

1 ounce capers (about 2 tablespoons)

salt

pepper

Place the cauliflower in a large pot and cover with water. Bring to a boil, reduce the heat, and simmer 15 for minutes. Remove from the heat, and drain. Cut the cauliflower into bite-sized chunks.

Heat the olive oil in a large skillet over medium-high heat. Add the garlic and cook for 1 minute. Add the cauliflower chunks and cook for 5 minutes more until lightly browned. Remove from the heat. Stir in the capers, and season with salt and pepper to taste. Serve warm.

Serves 4.

Cecina Fritta *(Chickpea Fritters)*

IT IS HARD TO BELIEVE, with our rich modern pantries, that flour was once a luxury. But chestnuts were a good substitute source of starch and chickpeas provided both starch and protein. All of the little towns in Tuscany used to have market stands where some cheerful old lady would make chestnut cakes, chickpea fritters and a few other little snacks. In Montecatini we had an old lady named Marina. Hers was a place to hang out with other kids. For the price of 15 lira her wonderful treats were something even a poor kid could afford.

1 quart cold water
1 cup chickpea flour
1 teaspoon salt, plus more for serving

1 tablespoon finely chopped fresh parsley
olive oil, for deep frying
1 lemon, cut into wedges

In a large, nonstick saucepan, whisk together the water, chickpea flour, and 1 teaspoon salt. Bring the mixture to a boil over medium heat. Cook stirring frequently to prevent sticking, until the mixture thickens and pulls away from the bottom of the pan when you stir, 10 to 15 minutes. Remove from the heat and stir in the parsley.

Pour the chickpea batter into a nonstick loaf pan. Cover and refrigerate for about 2 hours or more. Turn out the chickpea loaf onto a cutting board, and thinly slice.

Preheat the olive oil in a deep pot or deep-fat fryer. Deep fry the chickpea slices in the hot oil until dark golden brown and very light and crispy, 2 to 3 minutes per side. Transfer to a platter covered with paper towels. Season the crisps with salt while they are still hot. Serve hot with the lemon wedges.

Serves 4.

Roast Veal

EVERY ITALIAN MOTHER learns to make roast veal. Sirio's sister, Clara, makes the best one I know. There are a few secrets to it. First it must cook a long time so that the veal stays juicy while getting more and more tender. Clara makes her veal in a pot on top of the stove. Just a little steam escapes, but as the hours go by the apartment fills up with a delicious aroma. You know it's done when the family can't stand to wait anymore.

1 ½ pounds veal shoulder roast, tied with butcher's twine
1 tablespoon unsalted butter, cut into six pieces
1 clove garlic, finely chopped, plus 1 whole clove garlic, peeled and halved
1 ½ teaspoons finely chopped fresh sage
½ teaspoon finely chopped fresh rosemary
¼ teaspoon salt, plus more for seasoning

¼ teaspoon pepper, plus more for seasoning
1 carrot, peeled and coarsely chopped
1 stalk celery, coarsely chopped
1 shallot, peeled and coarsely chopped
1 tablespoon olive oil
½ cup dry white wine

Preheat the oven to 400°F.

Make six 1-inch incisions in the fatty side of the veal roast, and insert a piece of butter into each hole. In a small bowl, combine the garlic, sage, rosemary, salt, and pepper. Rub the mixture over the fatty side of the roast. Place the meat in an enameled baking dish that is large enough to hold the roast snugly, fatty side up. Drizzle the olive oil on top. Sprinkle the carrot, celery, shallot, and halved garlic clove over the roast.

Cover the baking dish, and bake the roast, turning it every 30 minutes, until the internal temperature reaches 145 to 150°F, about 1 ½ hours. Transfer the roast to a clean cutting board, and let rest for 10 minutes.

Meanwhile, place the baking dish with its pan juices over high heat on the stove top. Add the wine, bring to a boil, and boil vigorously until the liquid has reduced to about 1 ¼ cups, about 5 minutes. Puree the sauce in a blender or press it through a sieve. Season with salt and pepper to taste.

Carve the veal into 4 slices. Pour any accumulated meat juices from the cutting board into the sauce. Serve the meat immediately with the sauce on the side.

Serves 4.

MY THREE SONS: MARCO

We used to make these with Mom. With three boys, that's dangerous because we would keep eating the chicken liver pâté as we made the crostini so it was a race to see if there would be any left for dinner guests. This recipe was kind of my father's litmus test for a true grown-up palate because it had all those yucky ingredients that children rarely like: liver, anchovies, occasionally some tripe. We boys made my dad proud with these. I especially loved helping Mom and hearing her sing to pass the time. She has such a pretty voice, more people should hear it.

Chicken Liver Crostini

My boys absolutely love this. I learned it from my Nonna Leonella. It was a must-have appetizer for any holiday gathering. It has also sold well for us in New York where Eastern European Jewish families keep their tradition of creamy, oniony, sautéed chicken livers.

$1/3$ cup olive oil

$3/4$ cup chopped onions

6 fresh sage leaves, finely chopped, or 1 tablespoon dried sage leaves

1 clove garlic, peeled and finely chopped

1 pound chicken livers, coarsely chopped

2 tablespoons white wine

1 teaspoon tomato paste dissolved in $1/2$ cup water

2 tablespoons butter

2 ounces capers, finely chopped (about $1/4$ cup)

2 ounces anchovies, finely chopped (about $1/4$ cup)

salt

pepper

hot pepper sauce or crushed red pepper (optional)

1 baguette or $1/2$ loaf Tuscan bread

In a heavy saucepan, heat the olive oil over medium-high heat. Add the onions, sage, and garlic and cook until the onions begin to soften, 3 to 4 minutes. Add the chicken livers, and simmer, stirring, until the livers pieces appear cooked on the outside, 2 to 3 minutes. Add the diluted tomato paste and the wine. Mix well. Continue simmering until the water evaporates, 30 to 40 minutes.

Remove the saucepan from the heat and stir in the butter until it melts. Then, add the capers and anchovies and mix well. Season with salt and pepper to taste (don't over-salt—the capers and anchovies can be very salty). Add hot sauce or crushed red pepper to taste if desired.

Slice the bread into small pieces, and toast lightly. Spoon a generous portion of the chicken liver mixture on top. Serve warm.

Note: The chicken liver mixture can be prepared up to a day or two ahead without the butter, capers, anchovies, salt and pepper (and hot sauce if used). When ready to use, gently reheat the mixture on low heat, toast the bread, and add the remaining ingredients just before serving.

Serves 4.

Farro Pesto del Menesini *(Mensini's Farro with Pesto)*

FARRO IS A GRAIN that they served a lot in Lucca, which is about twenty miles from Montecatini, but I have only started to cook with it in the past fifteen years. It tastes and looks somewhat like barley. This recipe was perfected by one of our friends and a great figure in Tuscan cuisine, Renzo Menesini. Renzo was a professor at the local university. He specialized in herbs, in particular herbs and plants that eased pain. He would spend three months of the year in Thailand where he collected plants for his studies. At home in Tuscany, his house was filled with art. It had a great wine cellar and pork aging on marble slabs suspended in birdcages so that the animals couldn't get to the meat. Renzo was always involved with a beautiful woman. This was a man who loved food and all the senses.

Pesto

1 cup extra-virgin olive oil
$^1/_2$ cup pine nuts
4 cups fresh basil leaves

4 cloves garlic
$^3/_4$ cup grated Parmesan cheese
salt

Put all the ingredients except the salt in a blender or food processor. Mix well but do not puree—the basil leaves should be well broken up into tiny bits, and you should be able to see bits of the pine nuts. Incorporate salt to taste.

Makes about 2 $^1/_2$ cups pesto.

Farro

1 cup whole-grain farro (also called spelt)
2 cups water
$^1/_2$ cup Pesto (see recipe above)

Soak the farro in the water for 24 hours.

Drain. Put the farro in a medium saucepan, and cover with cold water. Bring to a boil on high heat. Cover, reduce the heat, and simmer for 20 minutes. Drain, and rinse in cold water. Drain well.

Toss the farro with the pesto.

Makes 2 cups.

Stuffed Cabbage

EVERY GOOD COOK in Montecatini tries to make this dish, but it takes some skill. Giovanna, my mother, made a stuffed cabbage that invariably used up every leftover in the house. I think the leftovers are what sold my boys on this dish, because cabbage is not always a child's favorite.

$\frac{1}{3}$ pound ground veal
$\frac{1}{4}$ pound prosciutto
$\frac{3}{4}$ cup grated Parmesan cheese
1 large white onion, peeled
2 medium carrots, peeled
1 large stalk celery
1 egg

2 tablespoons finely chopped
  fresh parsley or
  1 tablespoon dried parsley
$\frac{1}{2}$ clove garlic
1 to 2 pinches grated nutmeg
salt
freshly ground pepper

$\frac{1}{4}$ cup all-purpose flour
$\frac{1}{3}$ to $\frac{1}{2}$ cup olive oil
$\frac{3}{4}$ cup canned tomatoes
1 cup water
$\frac{1}{4}$ cup white wine
1 tablespoon red wine vinegar

Place the whole cabbage, stem side down, in a large pot. Fill the pot with water half way to the top of the cabbage. Cover and bring to a boil. Reduce the heat and simmer just until the cabbage barely begins to soften, 5 to 10 minutes. Drain off the water, and let the cabbage cool.

When cool enough to handle, very, very carefully part the leaves of the cabbage until you can reach in and scoop out the center one third to one half at the core of the cabbage, leaving the outer leaves attached. Set aside.

In a food processor, combine the veal, prosciutto, Parmesan, onion, carrots, celery, egg, parsley, and garlic. Pulse until well mixed but not pureed. Season with the nutmeg, and the salt and pepper to taste.

Carefully stuff the hollowed-out cabbage with the meat mixture, and gently press the leaves back together to close it well. Tie the cabbage head together with kitchen twine to hold it closed. Dust the entire head with the flour. In a large skillet, heat the olive oil over medium heat, add the cabbage, and cook it briefly for 5 minutes.

Return the cabbage to the large pot, stem side down. Carefully put the tomatoes around the cabbage, and pour in the water, wine, and vinegar. Cover the cabbage and cook for 1 hour over medium heat. Remove the twine. Serve warm.

Serves 4–6.

Gamberoni (*Jumbo Shrimp with Beans*)

THERE COULD BE nothing more simple than this: fresh beans, freshly caught shrimp, and some good olive oil to bring out all the flavor. When I made baccalà for Sirio and myself, my boys, like typical youngsters, didn't want any "stinky fish." They would say "No, Daddy, don't make us eat that." So these nice plump shrimp kept them happy. Actually Mauro liked the baccalà but Marco was less venturesome. It's the same with the grandchildren. Young Luke will eat anything Grandma makes, but with Olivia it is pizza, pasta, pizza.

½ pound dried cannellini (Great Northern) beans
1 sprig fresh sage
1 clove garlic, peeled and halved
20 jumbo shrimp for a main course
   (or 12 jumbo shrimp for an appetizer),
   deveined and peeled except for the tail

¼ cup extra-virgin olive oil
salt
pepper

Soak the beans in water overnight. Strain off the water and add fresh water along with the sage and garlic. Bring to boil, and cook until the beans are soft but not mushy. Strain off the water, and discard the sage and garlic. Set aside the beans.

Grill the shrimp until just cooked, 3 to 5 minutes. In a medium bowl, toss the shrimp with the beans and olive oil until well mixed and coated with the oil. Season with salt and pepper to taste. Serve warm or cold.

Serves 4.

Polenta a Bocconi

I THINK LAYERS MAKE this dish so interesting. You spread ragu on the bottom of a ramekin or small dish, then you put on a layer of polenta, then more ragu, more polenta and, finally, another layer of ragu and parmesan cheese on top. The result is meaty richness and the smooth creaminess of polenta. The boys would smile when they ate this and they would finish it up, making the same clinking sound with their spoons at the end that you make when you finish a crème caramel, trying to get every last bit.

Sauce

¼ pound dried mushrooms
2 tablespoons olive oil
½ pound ground pork or
    sausage meat
1 medium red onion, peeled
    and coarsely chopped

2 cups crushed tomatoes
¼ cup chicken stock
½ teaspoon salt
pinch pepper

Polenta

4 cups water
¾ cup milk
1 teaspoon salt
1 cup yellow cornmeal
1 cup grated Parmesan cheese
4 tablespoons butter

FOR THE SAUCE:
Soak the mushrooms in water for 20 to 30 minutes. Drain well, and squeeze out as much water as possible. Discard the water, and coarsely chop the mushrooms. In a large skillet or saucepan, heat the olive oil on medium-high heat. Add the mushrooms, pork, and onion and cook for 3 to 5 minutes, until the onion begins to soften and the meat begins to brown. Add the tomatoes, chicken stock, salt, and pepper. Cover and simmer for 30 minutes. Remove from the heat and set aside.

FOR THE POLENTA:
Preheat the oven to 350°F. Grease a non-stick 9-by-13-inch baking pan. Bring the water and milk to a boil in a large, nonstick pan. Add the salt. Reduce the heat to a simmer. Add the cornmeal very slowly, stirring constantly and rapidly to avoid lumps, until thoroughly incorporated. Simmer, stirring frequently, for a total of about 45 minutes from the time you started adding the cornmeal. The polenta should still be very loose. Remove from the heat and stir in 1 tablespoon Parmesan cheese and 2 tablespoons butter, until thoroughly incorporated.

Spoon one quarter of the polenta into the prepared pan and spread it out evenly over the bottom. Carefully spread one quarter of the meat sauce over the polenta and sprinkle 1 tablespoon Parmesan on top. Repeat with 3 more layers. Cut the remaining 2 tablespoons butter into small chunks, and sprinkle them on the very top.

Bake for 30 minutes. Serve warm with remaining Parmesan cheese.

Serves 8.

Stinco di Vitello *(Veal Shank)*

IN AMERICA, osso bucco is made in the Milanese style, with tomatoes and sometimes prosciutto. This is a simpler classic veal shank recipe, just as tender, but with just a few ingredients so that the deep flavor of the veal comes out fully. I always say that the secret ingredient is passion. You must cook passionately, letting the veal brown, creating a gorgeous color. It always takes time. The leftovers from this are marvelous in polpette.

1 whole veal shank (3 to 4 pounds)
¼ cup all-purpose flour
⅓ cup olive oil
2 cups veal broth or chicken broth
1 carrot, peeled

1 stalk celery
3 cloves garlic, peeled
2 bay leaves
½ cup white wine

Roll the veal shank in the flour until it is well coated. In a large skillet, heat the olive oil over medium-high head. Add the veal shank and cook for 5 to 10 minutes, turning it to brown all over.

Put the veal shank in a large, deep pan (big enough to accommodate the shank with its lid on) with the veal broth, onion, carrot, celery, garlic, and bay leaves. Make sure the level of the liquid comes halfway up the shank. Add water if necessary to bring the liquid to the correct level. Bring to a boil. Reduce the heat and simmer, covered, for 1 hour and 45 minutes, adding water if necessary to keep the appropriate level of liquid and periodically turning the veal to submerge all portions of the shank over the course of cooking it.

Add the wine, cover, and cook for 15 minutes longer. Transfer the shank to a warm platter and cover it to keep it warm. Bring the juices to a full boil and boil just until they begin to thicken. Strain the juices, discarding the vegetables. Season the veal and the juices with salt and pepper to taste. Serve the veal and juices warm.

Serves 4.

Spaghetti con Gamberetti *(Spaghetti with Shrimp)*

I DREAMED UP THIS DISH in America, but I was thinking of Italy. People are often surprised to find curry in Tuscan recipes, but when I tell them that Italian merchants were trading with India six hundred years ago, they get the picture. One evening Sirio and I were having dinner in Cinqueterre on the Ligurian Sea. They served us spaghetti with curry sauce. The idea of adding some sweet little shrimps to it came to me in New York, but the feeling the dish evokes is the one I had that day with my husband in Liguria.

$1/3$ cup olive oil

1 large white onion, peeled and finely chopped

1 small apple, cored, peeled, and thinly sliced

1 tablespoon finely chopped fresh parsley

$1/2$ pound small shrimp, peeled and deveined

1 teaspoon curry powder

2 tablespoons white wine

$3/4$ pound spaghetti

In a large skillet over medium heat, heat the olive oil. Add the onion and apple and cook until the apples just begin to soften. Add the parsley, and cook for 1 minute. Add the shrimp and the curry, increase the heat to medium-high, and cook just until the shrimp turn orange and opaque, 7 to 10 minutes.

Meanwhile, in a large pot of boiling, salted water, cook the spaghetti until al dente, about 12 minutes. Drain. Combine the shrimp mixture with the spaghetti and serve immediately.

Serves 4.

SIRIO SPEAKS

Alberto always hoped that I would follow in his footsteps and become a butcher. When he came to visit us in America he was very impressed when he saw how big and grand Le Cirque was. But that didn't change his mind. He looked at the restaurant, looked at me and said, "Can you just imagine, if you followed me in Italy you would have been the King of Salami!"

Maccheroni al Sugo di Salsiccia *(Pasta with Sausage Sauce)*

A TRUE PEASANT DISH and one that you can make very fast (I suppose this comes from the peasants having to hurry back to work in the fields). Sausage is inexpensive and usually on hand. Throw in some tomatoes, garlic and onions and you're done. In Italy we were very fond of the sausage that Sirio's uncle, Alberto, made. Once when Alberto came to visit us, my Uncle Renato took him to the races at Aqueduct. It is a beautiful track with a very pretty overhang to protect the spectators from the sun and the rain. Alberto spent a long time looking at it, even when the races were going on. Finally he turned to Renato and said, "This would be a terrific place to dry sausages."

2 tablespoons olive oil
1 large red onion, finely chopped
2 sweet Italian sausages, finely chopped
3 cloves garlic, peeled and finely chopped
2 tablespoons white wine

2 cups peeled and crushed tomatoes
salt
black pepper
crushed red pepper
1 pound pasta (any chunky shape)

In a medium saucepan, heat the olive oil over medium-high heat. Add the onion and sausages and cook until the sausage meat is just cooked through, about 5 minutes. Add the garlic and cool for 2 minutes. Add the wine and cook for 2 minutes. Add the tomatoes and season with salt, black pepper, and crushed red pepper to taste. Reduce the heat to low and simmer for 30 minutes.

In a pot of boiling, salted water, cook the pasta until al dente according to the directions on the package. Drain.

Toss the pasta with the sausage sauce and serve immediately.

Serves 4.

Frittata di Cipolle *(Onion Frittata)*

NONNA LEONELLA made this, so did Nonna Augusta. The frittata is a perfect recipe for presenting leftovers. Onions, which are the base of this dish, always develop a tempting aroma and a creamy sweetness. With salad and a crisp cold Pinot Grigio you have a terrific light lunch.

6 eggs
2 tablespoons grated Parmesan cheese
2 sprigs fresh parsley, finely chopped (about 1 teaspoon)
salt

pepper
olive oil
1 large white onion, peeled and thinly sliced
4 small zucchini, thinly sliced

In a large bowl, combine the eggs, Parmesan, and parsley. Season with salt and pepper to taste. Beat well, then set aside.

In a 9- or 10-inch, heavy, nonstick skillet, heat the olive oil over medium-high heat. Add the onion and zucchini and cook until they begin to soften, 4 to 5 minutes.

Spread the vegetables evenly over the bottom of the skillet. Pour the egg mixture on top of the vegetables, spreading it evenly. Reduce the heat to medium, and cook (without stirring) until the eggs are firm on top. Carefully flip the frittata using a large lid or plate to help you cook the other side for 1 to 2 minutes. Serve immediately, or refrigerate and serve cold.

Serves 4.

Stuffed Squab

IN OUR FIRST FEW YEARS in America I used to make squab for Thanksgiving. Its rosy meat has the scent of wild game that has foraged on autumn fruits and seeds. For years Americans looked at squab as "restaurant food." Now, with the current trend for game and more unusual foods, it has found its way into more and more homes for special occasions.

6 squabs
$\frac{1}{4}$ pound veal, cubed
$\frac{1}{4}$ pound sweet Italian sausage meat
$\frac{1}{4}$ pound chicken livers
$\frac{1}{4}$ pound thinly sliced mortadella ripped into
    1-inch pieces
$\frac{1}{4}$ pound chestnuts, peeled and roasted
$\frac{1}{4}$ pound Parmesan cheese, grated
1 small white onion, peeled and finely chopped
1 clove garlic, peeled
1 small egg

1 slice any plain bread
2 tablespoons finely chopped fresh parsley
2 tablespoons olive oil
1 tablespoon white wine
1 tablespoon butter
2 teaspoons milk
$\frac{1}{4}$ ounce black truffle (or as much as you can afford),
    peeled and very finely chopped
pinch salt
pinch pepper
pinch ground nutmeg

Preheat the oven to 350°F. Grease a 13-by-9-inch baking dish. Clean the squabs, reserving the livers and giblets.

In a food processor, combine the reserved livers and giblets along with all of the remaining ingredients. Pulse until well combined but not pureed.

Fill the cavities of the squabs with the stuffing. Tie the squabs with butcher's twine. Place them in the prepared baking dish and bake for 1 hour. Serve warm.

Serves 6.

Schiacciata

THIS IS MY FATHER'S RECIPE. When my boys used to take their lunch to school I would include schiacciata for them. One day I would send some with a thermos of minestrone. Another day, they would have it with chicken cacciatore or tortellini—"real food" to my Tuscan way of thinking. But my boys were in a New York school and wanted to feel like the other American kids. Also, my food was a little more appealing to their classmates than their ham and cheese or tuna-fish sandwiches. One day young Mario came home and said, "Mom, can you pack 'regular food' for my lunchbox, because the other kids eat up the stuff you give me, I get nothing and they all tease me!"

pizza dough (see recipe, page 27)
salt
$1/2$ cup olive oil

Preheat the oven to 350°F. Grease two 13-inch round pizza pans or two baking sheets.

Put each ball of pizza dough on one of the prepared pans. Pat and press the dough with your fingers to cover the bottom of the pans, rim to rim. Cover and let sit in a warm spot for 30 minutes.

Using two fingers of each hand, make random indentations in the surface of the dough in both pans. Sprinkle liberally with salt, and drizzle $1/4$ cup olive oil over each.

Bake the pizza breads for 15 minutes, or until golden brown. Transfer the pans as close as possible to the bottom of the oven (the oven floor or the lowest rack). Bake for 5 minutes longer to crisp the bottom crust. Cut into any size or shape you desire, and serve hot.

Serves 12.

My Turkey Stuffing

WE DIDN'T really have stuffed turkey in Italy. We would stuff pheasant, though, or a couple of chickens. So when it came time for me to stuff a Thanksgiving turkey in America, I adapted our Italian flavors to this American bird. Since our chestnuts in Montecatini are the best in Italy, I wouldn't think of making it without them. Then plain sausage, with fennel, salt, and pepper. Mauro always eats the most stuffing, but little Luke is showing every sign of following in his uncle's footsteps.

1 small turkey (about 10 pounds), deboned
3 slices any plain bread
$1/4$ cup milk
$1/2$ cup chopped fresh parsley
$1/2$ cup olive oil
$1\,1/2$ pounds veal, cubed
$1\,1/3$ pounds sweet Italian sausage meat
1 pound chicken livers

3 medium white onions, finely chopped
6 cloves garlic
$1/3$ cup white wine
1 pound thinly sliced mortadella, ripped into 1-inch pieces
3 eggs
1 pound chestnuts, peeled and roasted
1 pound Parmesan cheese, grated

1 ounce black truffle (or as much as you can afford), peeled and finely chopped
salt
pepper
ground nutmeg
4 tablespoons butter, softened

Refrigerate the turkey while you proceed. Preheat the oven to 400 F.

Put the bread and milk in the bowl of a large standing mixer. Let sit for 5 minutes. Add the parsley and mix to combine the ingredients and break the bread into tiny pieces. Set aside.

In a large saucepan, heat the olive oil on medium-high heat. Add the veal, sausage, chicken livers, onion, and garlic and cook, stirring occasionally, until the onions soften and all the meat pieces are cooked on the outside, about 20 minutes. Add the wine and cook for 10 minutes. Remove from the heat and let cool for about 10 minutes.

Add the contents of the saucepan to the bread mixture and mix well. Add the mortadella and eggs and mix well. Add the chestnuts, Parmesan, and truffles and mix well. Season with salt, pepper, and nutmeg to taste. Add the butter and mix until it is well incorporated into the stuffing.

With fine butcher's twine and a needle, sew the neck of the turkey closed. Pack the stuffing into the deboned inner cavity of the turkey. With the twine and needle, sew the rear of the turkey closed. Salt the outside of the turkey.

Place the stuffed turkey, breast side up, onto a rack in a large roasting pan. Cook for $1\,1/2$ to 2 hours, until the internal temperature reaches 170 F. Remove from oven, and let sit for 10 minutes before slicing.

Serves 10 to 12.

My Three Sons: Mario

When I think of big family meals, I will always remember the gatherings at the farm where my father grew up. It was a very simple place. The cooking was done in the kitchen fireplace. Once we bought a stove and a refrigerator for my Uncle Alberto, who still lived there. But they just gathered dust. Alberto believed in shopping for food the day you needed it and as for cooking, a fireplace was the only proper way. My dad had very few family members. The war had been hard on what had been a small family to begin with, but they always had this farm and that was his connection to his past. So gathering friends and family there was very important to him. It fell on my mother and Aunt Clara to organize these banquets. There would be thirty or forty people there, eating outside in the backyard. We had roasts, stews, pizza, butter, and sage raviolis, salads and castanaccia for dessert. After five minutes of gobbling food, the kids would all get up from the table and explore the farm and invariably someone took a fall and all the mothers and aunts would rush to make sure that we children survived.

Salsa de Menesini

I CANNOT THINK OF THIS SAUCE without remembering our friend Renzo Menesini. We would sit on the terrace of his ultramodern house which was so different-looking than the redone Tuscan villas that all the English and Americans spend so much on. Renzo didn't want a museum. He wanted a functional, ultra high tech and comfortable place to live and cook. This recipe is reminiscent of the sauce for vitello tonnato, but a little lighter and brighter. Great on crostini with a glass of Friulian white wine.

1 6-ounce can tuna, drained
3 ounces pitted green olives
3 ounces anchovies, drained
1/4 cup capers
1 tablespoon fresh lemon juice

1 clove garlic
pepper
olive oil
Focaccia or toasted Tuscan bread, for serving

In a food processor, combine the tuna, olives, anchovies, capers, lemon juice, and garlic. With the machine on, add the olive oil a little at a time until you achieve a paste the consistency of thick jam. Season with pepper to taste. Serve with warm focaccia or toasted Tuscan bread.

Makes about 1 1/2 cups.

Orange Tart

ONE DAY, CRAIG CLAIBORNE was coming for dinner. Sirio looked up from the newspaper and said "Egidiana, why don't you try oranges instead of apples in your tart?" Sirio has good cooking ideas even if he rarely gets to bring them to life on a stove (although he does fine whenever he tries). So I went to work on his suggestion and even though oranges are a lot more watery than apples, this worked out fine the first time.

Most mom's have a recipe for a pie crust. Lots of sugar, butter, eggs. One day I thought I would try for a little more tart taste so I added extra lemon juice and I liked the result. My boys did too. On Christmas I would take the leftover pastry and bake it into star shaped cookies.

Pie Pastry

1 cup plus 2 tablespoons all-purpose flour
$\frac{1}{3}$ cup sugar
grated zest of $\frac{1}{2}$ lemon (about $\frac{1}{4}$ teaspoon)
2 egg yolks
5 tablespoons butter, melted and cooled

Filling

2 large seedless oranges, ends trimmed and discarded and cut crosswise $\frac{1}{8}$ inch thick
1 lemon, ends trimmed and discarded and cut crosswise $\frac{1}{8}$ inch thick
$\frac{1}{4}$ cup sugar
$\frac{1}{4}$ cup Grand Marnier
$\frac{1}{2}$ cup orange marmalade, melted

FOR THE PASTRY:
Grease a 9- or 10-inch springform pan and dust lightly with flour. Set aside. In a medium bowl, combine the flour, sugar, and lemon zest with a whisk. Add the egg yolks, one at a time, whisking well after each addition. Slowly add the butter, whisking constantly. Blend the pastry with your hands, kneading it until it is homogenous and smooth.

Put the pastry dough in the center of the prepared pan. Press it out to cover the bottom of the pan and a little of the sides. Smooth the dough as much as possible. Cover and refrigerate until ready to use.

FOR THE FILLING:
Preheat the oven to 500°F. Prepare two baking sheets with sides, covering the bottom of each pan with a sheet of parchment paper.

Place the orange slices in a single layer on the prepared sheets. Remove the seeds from the lemon slices and place them in a single layer on the prepared sheets. Sprinkle with the sugar and Grand Marnier.

Bake the orange slices in the preheated oven for 2 minutes. Then reduce the temperature to 375°F,
(recipe continued on page 126)

without opening the oven door. Cook for 15 minutes more. Flip over the slices and cook for 10 to 15 minutes longer, watching carefully to make sure they do not burn, until they are sticky and a bit crisp. Remove from the baking sheets immediately so that they stop cooking and do not stick. Increase the temperature to 400 F.

Carefully arrange the orange slices on the prepared pastry, overlapping the edges in concentric circles. Choose the five prettiest lemon slices, and arrange them in an overlapping circle in the center (discard the remaining lemon slices). Carefully brush the melted marmalade over the arranged slices. Bake the tart at 400 F for 5 minutes. Then reduce the temperature to 350 F and bake 25 to 35 minutes longer, watching carefully to prevent burning. Let cool before serving.

NOTE: Be careful not to slice the lemons and oranges too thin or they will burn too easily.

Serves 6 to 8.

My Three Sons: Marco

One day I walked into the old Le Cirque and there was Frank Zappa chowing down on my mom's fritelle. I couldn't believe that this major hippie figure was eating in the same restaurant that President Nixon used to come to, but there he was. He had become a regular and he and my dad were great friends, but their friendship started out funny. Zappa came into the restaurant with his long hair and van Dyke and no tie. Dad had no idea who Zappa was. Dad took long-haired guys like Zappa as the ultimate challenge, so my father asked him if he wanted to try one of the ties we kept for this situation. He chose the ugliest yellow tie with big blue polka dots. At the end of the lunch, Zappa said, "Do you think I can borrow this tie? I have to go for an interview." My Dad told him to take it. Later that night I was watching David Letterman and there is Frank Zappa in the yellow tie. Letterman says, "Nice tie, Frank" and Zappa starts into this long story about how he went to this place uptown and had a wonderful lunch and how they made you wear a tie and there was this wonderful guy, Sirio. "And the nicest thing is," Zappa said in conclusion, "they give you the tie!"

Stuffed Pear Shaped Tomatoes

MY KIDS LOVE THESE. You cut the tomatoes, squeeze out the water, add some parsley, garlic, bread crumbs, and pepperoncini. It is a very versatile side dish. My youngest, Mario, especially loves it and even now that he is the biggest restaurateur in Las Vegas, whenever I go to visit it is the first thing he requests. When his older brother Marco was little, he too could always be counted on to eat anything with tomatoes. Meat was a different story with Marco. He would only pretend to eat it, as I found out when I was cleaning under the table. Marco had stuck a few meals worth of meat there, cut up in little pieces.

10 pear or plum shaped tomatoes
$^3/_4$ cup finely chopped fresh parsley
3 cloves garlic, peeled
pinch crushed red pepper

$^3/_4$ cup plain bread crumbs or 1 $^1/_2$ slices white bread
1 cup olive oil
salt
pepper

Preheat the oven to 400 F. Pour about $^1/_2$ cup water in the bottom of a nonstick 9-by-13-inch baking pan. Set aside.

Cut the tomatoes in half lengthwise. Scoop out and discard the liquid and seeds in the center of the tomatoes. Set aside the scooped-out tomatoes.

In a food processor, combine the parsley, garlic, crushed red pepper, bread crumbs or bread, $^1/_2$ cup olive oil, and salt and pepper to taste, pulsing until the ingredients are well chopped but not blended or pureed. Spoon this mixture into the prepared tomato halves. Drizzle the remaining $^1/_2$ cup olive oil on top of the stuffed tomatoes, and carefully transfer them to the prepared baking pan.

Cover the pan with aluminum foil and bake the tomatoes for 45 minutes. Remove the foil and place the pan under the broiler for 2 to 3 minutes until the tomatoes are slightly brown on top. Serve warm.

Serves 4.

Fritelle di Riso (*Rice Fritters*)

THESE ARE THE TRADITIONAL SWEETS for Saint Joseph's Day (March 19). Nonna Augusta and I would make a lot of them and eat them all day. We have them hot at lunchtime, cold at dinnertime, but always delicious.

1 cup rice	3 tablespoons sugar	3/4 cup all-purpose flour
2 cups milk	zest of 1 lemon	4 eggs
1 3/4 cups water, divided	3 tablespoons butter	vegetable oil, for deep frying

Put the rice, milk, 1 cup water, sugar, and lemon zest in a medium saucepan. Bring to a boil over high heat. Let the mixture cook until the liquid is absorbed, 30 to 40 minutes. Remove from the heat and set aside.

In a small saucepan, bring the remaining 3/4 cup water to a boil with the butter. Add the flour, and mix well. Remove from the heat. Add the eggs, one at a time, beating vigorously after each addition with a sturdy whisk.

Once all the eggs are mixed, combine the flour mixture with the rice. Form patties of 1 rounded tablespoonful each.

Preheat the vegetable oil in a deep pot or deep-fat fryer. Deep fry the patties in the very hot oil until dark golden brown. Transfer to a platter covered with paper towels. Serve warm or cool.

Makes about 24 fritters.

Apple Tart of Mama Giovanna

MOST PEOPLE remember their mother's apple pie from childhood. This is, indeed, my mother's apple pie (actually it is her cousin Velleda's recipe). My mother would make the pie crust and fill it and bring it downstairs to the bakery where my dad would bake it. My father was the dessert man. I remember one year, for my mother's birthday on the tenth of July, he made a big pot of homemade ice cream. He turned and turned the ice-cream maker for what seemed hours—but, then, waiting for ice cream if you are a child can make minutes seem like hours. When it was done we invited all the neighbors and had an ice-cream party in honor of my mother.

Crust

bread crumbs, for dusting
1 stick (4 ounces) plus 2 tablespoons
    butter, softened
½ cup sugar
1 cup all-purpose flour

1 teaspoon baking powder
2 eggs, lightly beaten
¼ cup milk
zest of ½ lemon
    (about ¼ teaspoon)

Filling

2 pounds apples
juice of 1 lemon
¼ cup sugar
3 tablespoons butter, melted
2 tablespoons bread crumbs
chilled whipped cream, for topping

FOR THE CRUST:
Preheat the oven to 325°F. Generously grease a 10- to 12-inch pie pan. Sprinkle the entire pan with bread crumbs. Set aside.

In a large bowl, cream the butter and sugar together. Sift the flour and baking powder together, and add to the butter mixture, combining well. Add the eggs, milk, and lemon zest. Combine well to create a soft dough. Spoon the dough into the prepared pan, and press with the back of a large spoon or your hand until the dough is flat and evenly covers the bottom and sides of the pan. Set aside.

FOR THE FILLING:
Peel and thinly slice the apples. Toss with the lemon juice. Mix the apples with the sugar, butter, and bread crumbs. Dump the apple mixture into the unbaked pie shell. Gently shake the pan a few times to even them out.

Bake the pie for about 1 hour, until the apples have softened when tested in their center with a toothpick. Then put the pie under the broiler for about a minute, just to brown the apples, being careful not to burn them.

Serve the pie slightly warm with a generous helping of chilled whipped cream.

NOTE: Once the tart is thoroughly cooked, you can remove it from the oven and set it aside, then broil the top immediately before serving.

Serves 8.

Montebianco

A CHRISTMAS DESSERT that looks like a snow-covered mountain. I learned it from an old pastry chef in Montecatini in the oldest pastry shop in town. The shop is still there, but the baker, Giovanni, is probably creating desserts for angels at this point. My boys loved the mountain shape. Marco used to help me make this when he was young, then Mauro took over, but Mario never became a dessert maker.

2 pounds chestnuts, peeled and roasted
1 ½ quarts milk
1 teaspoon vanilla extract
1 ½ cups granulated sugar

3 tablespoons rum
1 quart heavy cream
2 cups confectioners' sugar

In a medium saucepan, bring the chestnuts, milk, and vanilla to a boil over medium-high heat. Cook until the chestnuts are soft enough to mash with a fork, 25 to 30 minutes. Strain off and reserve the milk and chestnuts separately.

Combine the granulated sugar and rum with the chestnuts. Press the mixture through a ricer or food mill. The texture should be that of a soft paste. Add a little of the reserved milk, if needed, to obtain this texture. Discard the remaining milk.

On a small platter, make a mountain shape with the chestnut paste. Chill it if you will not be eating it right away.

Just before serving, whip the cream until it forms stiff peaks. Quickly whip in the confectioners' sugar.

Top the mountain with the whipped cream. Serve immediately.

Serves 8.

Torta Egi al Cioccolato *(Egi's Chocolate Cake)*

THIS IS NOT a Tuscan recipe but I love it anyway. It is inspired by the Torta Caprese, a famous chocolate and almond cake of Capri. My boys liked it when they were growing up and they still like it. I often make this instead of chocolate-chip cookies. It's faster and what's more, it is Italian.

3 egg yolks

1 1/4 cups confectioners' sugar

1 stick (4 ounces) plus 3 tablespoons butter, softened

4 1/2 ounces bittersweet chocolate, melted

1/2 pound almonds, very finely ground

1 tablespoon all-purpose flour

5 egg whites, very stiffly beaten

Preheat the oven to 325 F. Grease an 8- or 9-inch round baking pan and set aside. In a medium bowl, beat the egg yolks and sugar together. Add the butter and beat until well combined. Slowly beat in the melted chocolate. Then, add the ground almonds and flour and combine well. Gently fold in the egg whites, just until well incorporated into the mixture.

Gently pour the batter into the prepared pan. Bake the cake for 35 to 45 minutes until a cake tester inserted in the center of the cake comes out clean. Let the cake cool for 10 minutes on a rack. Then, gently turn the cake out onto a serving platter.

Serves 8.

restaurant

Restaurant

SIRIO SERVING
SUNDAY DINNER AT
OUR HOME TO MY
UNCLE RENATO
(LEFT) AND ALAIN
SAILHAC (RIGHT)

SIRIO AT THE
OLD LE CIRQUE

IN 1972 Sirio was working in the Pierre Hotel. It was a job, and for that one is always grateful, but it really wasn't suited to my husband. It was more of a nightclub with food. The late hours were a problem for a young father who wanted to spend time with his family. Also, Sirio had spent years as a maitre'd at the Colony, perhaps the greatest restaurant in New York. From Frank Sinatra to Cary Grant to Princess Grace, he had already developed a following among a very exclusive clientele. Sirio always had this great ability to make you feel pretty or important or special and it served him well. And then the most wonderful thing happened. Mr. William Zeckendorf, a major realtor and one of Sirio's regulars at the Colony proposed that Sirio take over the restaurant at the Mayfair House Hotel, which was one of Mr. Zeckendorf's properties. Sirio's attitude, and mine too, was why not? His charm and professionalism had won him the loyalty of the cream of society. He was young, polished, strong, ambitious and Mr. Zeckendorf pretty much took all of the financial risk. So Sirio invited a partner, Jean Verne, who had been a chef at the Colony and they had a deal where Sirio would take care of the dining room—what we in the restaurant business call "the front of the house"—and Jean would take care of the kitchen.

Although the money was tight and the work was tough, the place was an instant success. The Colony customers flocked to dine at their Tuscan charmer's new place. We started to be more financially secure, but to tell you the truth, as long as we had food and a home, the things that money can buy never interested me that much. I often say "if money were flowers then I could count them," but just counting money for the sake of money never interested me.

But the success was very gratifying. I will never forget when my mother came to Le Cirque for the first time. She remembered well a time years before in Italy when I was singing in a nightclub with the Casini Orchestra.

One time Sirio sat with us at this fancy nightclub and the owner came over and said, "It is forbidden. You cannot sit at the musicians' table." So Sirio got his own table and motioned for my mother and me to come over and he ordered a bottle of Dom Perignon!

In those days I didn't realize what an expensive gesture this was, but Sirio knew and he said, "Someday, I swear, I am going to have a beautiful place that makes this look like nothing!" My mother admired Sirio's spirit but honestly I think she felt it was just youth and wounded

MARCO AND ME
IN NEW YORK

MARCO, WITH ME
AND MARIO AT
LE CIRQUE

pride talking. Years later, when she came to visit us and saw Le Cirque she turned to me and said, "By God, Sirio was right!"

After nearly twenty years on Sixty-fifth Street, we had the opportunity to move Le Cirque to bigger quarters in the beautiful Villard Houses on Madison Avenue and at the same time we also had a business opportunity to open a Tuscan restaurant not far from there. My boys were all grown then and I too was looking for something to do so we opened Circo, a restaurant devoted to the recipes of Tuscany. I created the menu and the boys ran the restaurant. Very soon we had the chance to open restaurants in Las Vegas and Mexico City. Now the boys each have a restaurant to oversee. It's hard to believe that so much has happened in these past few years. And everywhere the Maccioni family goes, you will surely find haute cuisine alla francese, but you will just as surely find the recipes of Leonella and Augusta, Livia, Genoveffa, Giovanna, Clara, and Egi.

Liver and White Truffle Pâté

WHITE TRUFFLES are the most sought after gourmet food in Italy. I never tasted one when I was young, although my grandmother did. They used to have them in the mountains near Bologna. She loved them served very simply, shaved on top of scrambled eggs. In America, in recent years, white truffles have cost as much as $1,900 per pound. But don't worry, white truffle oil and white truffle paste are very affordable and you still get that wonderful earthy aroma in this pâté. Serve on crostini.

¼ cup olive oil
¼ cup finely chopped onion
½ pound chicken livers, cut in half with fat trimmed off and discarded
3 tablespoons Cognac

6 tablespoons butter, 4 tablespoons softened and 2 tablespoons melted
1 small white truffle, finely chopped (or 2 teaspoons white truffle puree)
small pieces of buttered toast or crackers

In a small skillet, heat the oil over medium heat. Add the onions and cook until very soft, 7 to 10 minutes. Add the chicken livers, reduce the heat to low, and simmer, covered, for 15 minutes. Remove from the heat. Add the Cognac and ignite it to burn off the alcohol. Let the mixture cool for 5 minutes. Then, transfer the mixture it to a food processor or blender, add the softened butter and the truffle, and blend until smooth.

Generously butter a small crock or soufflé pan, 5 to 6 inches in diameter. Spoon the liver mixture into the prepared crock. Press it down, and smooth the top. Pour the melted butter on top. Cover and refrigerate for at least 2 hours. Serve with buttered toast or crackers. (Leave the melted butter on top or remove it before serving, as you prefer.)

NOTE: After a portion of the pâté is consumed, add an additional layer of melted butter before returning to refrigerator to prevent discoloration.

Makes about 1 ½ cups pâté.

Clams Casino

Although my mother makes this, it's not really a recipe from Italy. She learned it from my Great Aunt Maria in Brooklyn, the wife of her Uncle Renato. I think Maria learned it from some guy in New Jersey. Mom would make it on rainy Sunday afternoons when we needed an activity. Whoever was around would pitch in, opening the clams, laying the bacon on top. I can remember some Sundays when Danny Kaye, who was a terrific cook, would come over and help, or Donald Sutherland, or the Italian actor and comedian Ugo Tognazzi. It was a real group effort because each one of us could easily eat two or three dozen of the sweet little clams apiece.

—MARCO

2 dozen littleneck clams, rinsed under running water for 15 to 20 minutes
1 tablespoon water
1 tablespoon olive oil, plus more for drizzling
1 slice white bread (any kind) crumbled in a food processor
2 tablespoons finely chopped fresh parsley
2 tablespoons very finely chopped red onion

2 teaspoons very finely chopped green bell pepper
1 clove garlic, minced
2 tablespoons butter, melted
salt
black pepper
crushed red pepper
6 slices bacon, each one divided into 4 pieces

Preheat the oven to 400 F.

Put the clams in a medium saucepan with the water and 1 tablespoon olive oil. Cover, and bring to boil. Simmer until the clams open, about 2 minutes. Remove from the heat immediately. (They will not be fully cooked.) Split the clams open and remove the meat, reserving all the shells, pan juices and the juices from the clams.

Combine the clams and the liquid together, and stir the clams around a bit to rinse them. Remove the clams and coarsely chop them. Set aside.

Strain the liquid through very fine cheesecloth to remove any grit and bits of shell. Combine the strained liquid with the clams, breadcrumbs, parsley, onion, green pepper, garlic, and butter. Season to taste with salt, black pepper, and crushed red pepper.

Pick out 2 dozen of the best-looking, largest clam shell halves. Stuff them with the clam mixture. Place a piece of bacon on top of each, and place them in a large baking dish in one layer. Drizzle all over with a little olive oil.

Bake for 15 to 20 minutes until the bacon appears fully cooked.

Serves 4.

Fried Zucchini Flowers

IF THERE IS ONE DISH that makes you a Tuscan, this would be it. Every cook in Tuscany makes zucchini flowers. I suppose my recipe is a combination of my mother's, my grandmother's, my aunt's and every other Tuscan woman I ever saw in the kitchen. I like to make my batter with beer. The results are super crispy.

16 zucchini flowers or squash blossoms
16 small shrimp, peeled and deveined
vegetable oil, for deep frying

$^1\!/_3$ cup all-purpose flour
1 recipe beer batter (see page 39)
salt

Clean the flowers by gently brushing off any visible dirt. Gently open each blossom, and remove the internal parts of the flower, leaving the petals and stem intact. Carefully insert one shrimp into each blossom, and close the petals around it.

Preheat the vegetable oil in a deep pot or deep-fat fryer. Dip each blossom in flour, shaking off any excess. Then, dip the floured blossom in the beer batter, making sure to coat the entire flower.

Deep fry the blossoms in the hot oil, just until they turn golden brown. Remove from the oil and sprinkle with salt immediately. Serve immediately.

Serves 4.

Pizza Margherita

ONE OF OUR FAVORITE PIZZAS. We have been serving it since we opened Circo. Our ovens are very hot in the restaurant so we are able to make it with a very thin crust. In the home oven it may be a little harder. I learned to make it from my father and he learned it because every baker in Italy knew this patriotic pizza. I say patriotic because the red tomatoes, white mozzarella and green basil are the colors of the Italian flag. That is why a pizzamaker named Raffaele Esposito made it for Queen Margherita of Savoy and because he was a gentleman, he named it after her.

pizza dough (see recipe, page 27)
$\frac{1}{2}$ cup olive oil
2 cups canned peeled tomatoes, well-drained and
   cut into half-inch pieces
$\frac{1}{2}$ pound mozzarella cheese, grated

1 teaspoon dried oregano
20 fresh basil leaves
salt
pepper

Pour 2 tablespoons olive oil into the center of each of two 13-inch pizza pans. Using lightly floured fingers, pat each ball of pizza dough into a thick round. Add one round of dough to the center of each pizza pan. Pat and press the dough to cover the bottom of the pans, rim to rim. Cover and let sit in a warm spot for about 30 minutes.

Preheat the oven to 400°F. Scatter equal amounts of the ingredients over each of the two pizzas in this order: tomato pieces, mozzarella, oregano, basil, the $\frac{1}{4}$ cup remaining olive oil, and salt and pepper to taste.

Place the pans in the oven and bake the pizzas until the crust is a deep golden brown, 25 to 30 minutes.

Serves 8.

Spaghetti al Mare *(Spaghetti with Shellfish)*

SIRIO AND I were once on the QE2 and the meal planners requested a recipe for spaghetti with seafood. I improvised something on the spot based on an Italian classic that Sirio and I used to love in Viareggio. I was singing there with Mauro Casini's band, real smoky ballads: "My Funny Valentine," "The Man I Love," "Summertime." I would sing whole songs in English, although at that time I didn't understand a word of it. The same went for songs in Spanish, Greek and French. I sang them all without a clue of what the words meant.

1 pound spaghetti
1 cup olive oil
4 cloves garlic, peeled and thinly sliced
pinch cayenne pepper
24 littleneck clams, rinsed under running water for 15 to 20 minutes
1 pound mussels, cleaned, beards removed

1 cup champagne
20 small to medium shrimp, peeled and deveined
4 plum tomatoes, peeled, seeded, and diced
$1/4$ cup coarsely chopped fresh parsley
1 tablespoon butter
salt
pepper

In a large pot of boiling, salted water, cook the spaghetti until al dente, 8 to 9 minutes. Drain and set aside to cool. (The spaghetti will finish cooking in the sauce.)

Heat $3/4$ cup olive oil in a large skillet over medium-high heat. Add the garlic and cayenne and simmer for 1 minute. Add the clams and cook for 1 minute. Add the mussels and champagne, cover the pan, and cook until all the clams and mussels have opened, 3 to 4 minutes. (If any of the shellfish refuse to open, discard them.) Drain, reserving the cooking liquid and the shellfish separately. Remove the shellfish from their shells. Discard the shells, and set the meat aside.

Heat the remaining $1/4$ cup olive oil in a large skillet over medium-high heat. Add the shrimp and cook until orange and nearly opaque, 2 to 3 minutes. Add the cooked clams and mussels, the tomatoes, the spaghetti, the reserved shellfish liquid, the parsley, and the butter. Season with salt and pepper to taste. Cook until all the ingredients are well combined and the spaghetti is well coated with the sauce. Serve immediately.

Serves 4.

Ricotta and Spinach Ravioli

NONNA AUGUSTA was a great ravioli maker. They were also a great favorite on our picnics in the hills on the day after Easter. When Le Cirque was on Sixty-fifth Street I would send twenty portions a day over to the restaurant. I had this super-secret and quite wonderful ravioli machine that I bought in Viareggio more than twenty years ago. In fact it was so great I bought two of them. Good thing, because when I loaned one to our chef, he messed up the handle. I took it right back and it has never left my house since. I tried to buy another one for the restaurant but it turned out that the man who made the originals had sold the mold to a competitor who broke the mold. My machines will now never leave my house!

Ravioli dough

2 cups all-purpose flour

3 eggs

1 teaspoon olive oil

¼ teaspoon salt

1 tablespoon finely chopped fresh parsley

¼ clove garlic, minced

freshly grated nutmeg

salt

pepper

Filling

½ cup ricotta cheese (fresh, if possible)

⅓ cup grated Parmesan cheese

⅓ cup cooked spinach, squeezed of excess water and finely chopped

Sauce

3 tablespoons butter, melted

16 to 20 fresh sage leaves

⅓ cup grated Parmesan cheese

pepper

FOR THE RAVIOLI DOUGH:
Combine all of the ingredients in a food processor and process to make a soft dough. Add a little flour if the dough is too sticky. Transfer the dough to a small bowl and refrigerate, covered, for 1 hour.

FOR THE FILLING:
In a large bowl, beat together the ricotta, Parmesan, spinach, parsley, and garlic until thoroughly combined. Season with the nutmeg, salt, and pepper to taste (make it a little extra salty since some of the saltiness will be lost when the ravioli are boiled). Set aside.

(recipe continued on page 148)

FOR THE TOPPING:
In a medium skillet, melt the butter over medium-low heat. Gently stir in the sage leaves. Set aside. (Best if done at the last minute before serving.)

ASSEMBLING THE RAVIOLI:
Fill a large soup pot three quarters full of water and bring to a boil.

Using a pasta machine, make rectangular strips as thin as possible from the ravioli dough. Cut the strips into 3- to 4-inch squares. Put a small spoonful of filling in the center of half of the squares. Be careful not to add too much filling, or the ravioli will not seal well. Cover the filled squares with the remaining dough squares. Press the edges of each ravioli firmly closed with your fingers or the tines of a fork. (If the dough does not stick, you can seal it with a little beaten egg.)

Cook the ravioli in the boiling water, stirring very gently only occasionally to make sure they do not stick to each other. Cook them to your preference, between 3 and 8 minutes.

FOR THE SAUCE:
Gently drain the ravioli and place in a warm serving bowl. Toss very gently with the butter and sage. Sprinkle with the Parmesan and pepper to taste. Serve immediately.

Serves 4.

Summer Pasta

ONE HOT SUMMER DAY in Tuscany, I wanted to make a quick meal for a lot of people but I didn't want to linger over the stove. This summer pasta with raw tomatoes and cubes of mozzarella that melt in the hot pasta worked beautifully. Just make sure the pasta is good and hot. When it is all done, toss with fresh basil.

½ pound fresh mozzarella cheese, finely diced
4 medium tomatoes, finely diced
½ cup coarsely chopped fresh basil
½ cup olive oil
2 cloves garlic, peeled and finely chopped

1 tablespoon kosher salt
black pepper
crushed red pepper
¾ pound spaghetti or penne rigate

In a large bowl, toss together the mozzarella, tomatoes, basil, olive oil, garlic, and salt. Season generously with black pepper and crushed red pepper. Cover and let sit for 30 minutes at room temperature.

In a large pot of boiling, salted water, cook the pasta until al dente according to the directions on the package. Drain. Toss immediately with the mozzarella/tomato mixture. (Or add a tablespoon of olive oil to the drained pasta, and let it come to room temperature before combining.)

Serves 4.

Lasagna Bolognese

Nonna Augusta would make this for holidays because it was a rich dish. As I have mentioned, in the past we distinguished between holiday dishes and everyday dishes. Christmas, Easter, Ferragosto: We would make this recipe, the three generations of women in the kitchen, Augusta, Momma, and me. I loved Ferragosto. It was a national recognition of the fact that nearly everyone took time off in August anyway. You would visit friends in nearby towns and have wonderful meals. And then sweet, ripe watermelons for dessert. My Uncle Giorgio would make a hole in the watermelon and drop some grappa and sugar inside. Then he would replace the plug, put the melon in an ice chest and it would be so cool and sweet, with a little extra kick from the grappa.

Meat Sauce

3/4 cup olive oil

1 small carrot, peeled and grated (about 3/4 cup)

1/2 stalk celery, finely chopped (about 1/2 cup)

1 medium red onion, peeled and finely chopped

1/3 pound ground beef

1/4 pound ground pork or veal

2 cups canned peeled tomatoes

2 tablespoons tomato paste

1/4 cup water

2 tablespoons butter

salt

pepper

Béchamel Sauce

1 cup milk

4 tablespoons butter

2 tablespoons all-purpose flour

pinch freshly grated nutmeg

salt

pepper

Lasagna dough

2 cups all-purpose flour, plus more if needed

3 eggs

1 teaspoon olive oil

1/4 teaspoon salt

Toppings

3/4 cup grated Parmesan cheese

1 tablespoon butter, cut into small pieces

For the meat sauce:

Heat the olive oil in a large pot over medium-high heat. Add the carrot, celery, and onion and cook for 2 minutes. Add the beef and pork and cook until the meat is nicely browned, 15 to 20 minutes. Add the canned tomatoes.

Dilute the tomato paste in the water. Add it to the meat sauce along with the butter and bring sauce to a simmer. Season with salt and pepper to taste. Cover, reduce the heat to the lowest setting, and cook, stirring occasionally, for about 1 hour. Remove from the heat and set aside.

FOR THE BÉCHAMEL SAUCE:

Combine the milk, butter, and flour in a small saucepan and slowly bring to a boil over medium heat. Reduce the heat to medium-low, and continue cooking until the mixture begins to thicken, about 2 minutes. Remove from the heat. Stir in the nutmeg, and season with salt and pepper to taste. Set aside.

FOR THE LASAGNA DOUGH:

Combine all the ingredients in a food processor until it makes a soft, but not sticky dough. Add a little more flour if the dough is too sticky. Transfer the dough to an airtight container and refrigerate for 1 hour.

Using a pasta machine, make long sheets as thin as you can make them. Let the sheets dry for a few minutes. Then cut them into sections, each about 13 inches long. Cook the lasagna in rapidly boiling water, stirring very gently to make sure they do not stick to each other, for about 2 minutes. Drain and rinse with cold water. Flatten them out on clean kitchen towels, and set aside until ready to use (no more than 30 minutes in advance).

Preheat oven to 350 F. Lightly grease a 13-by-9-inch baking pan.

Spoon one quarter of the meat sauce into the bottom of the prepared pan, and spread it around. Then, layer with: lasagna sheets, one-third of the béchamel, one-quarter of the meat sauce, and a little Parmesan. Repeat the layers two more times, and top with the remaining Parmesan and pieces of butter. Bake for 30 to 45 minutes, until the cheese begins to turn golden brown. Serve warm.

Serves 6.

Lasagnette di Verdure *(Vegetarian Lasagna)*

WHEN WE used to drive from Montecatini up to France, we would pass through hundreds of miles of a tunnel-filled route through the mountains that rise from the sea. Up near the border you'll find the town of Ventimiglia and a restaurant that we always stop at, Balzi Rossi. A lasagnette that we had there seven or eight years ago inspired this dish. You can use asparagus, but I like string beans. They get nice and soft with the potatoes. I don't understand this modern style of making crunchy string beans and asparagus. I am always fighting with my chefs about this. You must cook these vegetables until the fibers break down and release all the flavor.

Lasagna dough

1 ¾ cups all-purpose flour
2 eggs
2 tablespoons butter, softened

Vegetables

1 pound green beans
1 pound potatoes, peeled

Béchamel

1 stick (4 ounces) plus 2 tablespoons butter
⅓ cup all-purpose flour
2 ⅓ cups milk
1 teaspoon salt
1 to 2 pinches freshly grated nutmeg
1 cup grated Parmesan cheese
2 tablespoons butter, broken into small bits
salt
pepper

FOR THE LASAGNA DOUGH:
Combine all of the ingredients in a food processor and process to make a soft dough. Transfer the dough to a small bowl and refrigerate, covered, for 1 hour.

Using a pasta machine, make 13-inch sheets from the pasta dough. In a large pot of boiling water, cook the sheets of pasta for 2 to 3 minutes. Drain and set aside.

FOR THE VEGETABLES:
Trim and discard the ends of the green beans. Steam the beans for 5 to 6 minutes. Drain and set aside. Thinly slice the potatoes and steam for about 10 minutes. Drain and set aside.

FOR THE BÉCHAMEL:
In a medium saucepan, melt the butter over low heat. Whisk in the flour until well blended. Cook for 2 minutes, stirring. Slowly stir in the milk, salt and nutmeg. Increase the heat to

medium and bring to a boil. Cook, stirring constantly, just until it begins to thicken. Immediately remove from the heat and set aside.

ASSEMBLING THE LASAGNA:
Preheat the oven to 450 F. Grease a 9-by-13-inch pan. Spread one third of the vegetables on the bottom of the prepared pan. Cover with one third of the béchamel, $1/3$ cup Parmesan, and half the pasta sheets. Repeat the layers, making two separate layers of pasta but three layers of everything else, ending with Parmesan on top. Then scatter the butter on top and season with salt and pepper to taste.

Bake for 1 hour, until the cheese is a deep golden brown on top. Serve warm.

Serves 6 to 8.

MY THREE SONS: MAURO

When I am in Italy, I like to go to a restaurant in the middle of nowhere on a fall or winter day where they do a really good bollito misto. A few years ago, on the way back from skiing, it was cold and foggy when we stopped at a small place just outside Verona. From the outside it didn't look like anything special, but inside it was wonderful. Waiters with starched white jackets. Hefty old silverware. And in the middle of the dining room a bollito cart. They opened it up and the warm steam smelled delicious. Alongside the meats were the traditional mustard fruits, pickles, onions, salsa verde, and oversize salt and pepper shakers. Unforgettable.

Bollito Misto (*Mixed Boil*)

SOME YEARS AGO the famous Lyonnaise chef Paul Bocuse visited New York and Sirio begged me to do bollito misto for him. It is the Tuscan version of the French pot au feu or the Spanish cocido, a one-pot "everything" kind of meal. Bocuse loved it and after that this rustic farmer's dish became a weekly special for the high-society people who ate at Le Cirque.

There are two sauces that I serve with bollito misto representing the two parts of my heritage, the Tuscan and the Bolognese. The green sauce, from Nonna Augusta is full of fresh herbal flavor and snappy cornichons and capers that cut through the powerful meat flavors in bollito misto. The red sauce is from my mother and Nonna Leonella. It works well on pasta too. If I had to pick one it would be the green one because I like the sourness, but it turns out I never have to pick because we always serve both sauces.

Chicken sausage

2 pounds ground chicken (or 3 whole chicken breasts, skinned, deboned, and very finely chopped)

3 eggs

²/₃ cup mortadella, thinly sliced and ripped into small pieces (about ²/₃ cup)

¹/₂ cup grated Parmesan cheese

¹/₄ cup coarsely chopped flat-leaf parsley

1 clove garlic, finely chopped

1 teaspoon salt

¹/₂ teaspoon pepper

¹/₄ teaspoon grated nutmeg

Broth, Meat, and Vegetables

6 cups cold water

1 quart chicken broth

1 3- to 4-pound chicken

2 pounds beef shank

2 pounds beef short ribs

1 red onion, peeled

1 white onion, peeled

3 stalks celery

1 ripe tomato, halved

2 bay leaves

3 sprigs parsley

1 teaspoon salt, plus more to taste

4 black peppercorns, plus ground pepper to taste

4 carrots, peeled and cut into 2-inch pieces

4 potatoes, peeled and cut into 2-inch pieces

4 leeks, ends trimmed off, cut in half, and well cleaned

Minestra di semolina

3 eggs, lightly beaten

¹/₂ cup Cream of Wheat

¹/₄ cup grated Parmesan cheese

1 tablespoon milk, or more as needed

1 tablespoon butter, softened

1 teaspoon salt

¹/₂ teaspoon pepper

Condiments

¹/₂ cup green sauce (see recipe, page 157)

¹/₂ cup Tuscan red sauce (see recipe, page 157)

(recipe continued on pages 156–157)

FOR THE CHICKEN SAUSAGE:

In a large bowl, combine all of the ingredients and mix well. Shape the mixture into a log about 3 to 4 inches in diameter. Wrap the log securely in cheesecloth and tie it well with kitchen twine. Refrigerate until needed.

FOR THE BROTH, MEAT, AND VEGETABLES:

Place the water, chicken broth, beef shank and ribs, red and white onions, celery, tomato, bay leaves, parsley, salt, and peppercorns in a very large soup pot. Bring to a boil. Reduce the heat and simmer, covered, for 45 minutes. Add the prepared chicken sausage, and simmer for another 45 minutes. Add the carrots, potatoes, and leeks, and simmer for 30 minutes more.

Carefully transfer the carrots, potatoes, leeks, shank ribs, and chicken sausage from the broth to a large, warm platter. Drizzle a few large spoonfuls of broth on top of the vegetables and meat to keep them moist. Cover and let sit in a warm place until ready to serve.

Strain the remaining broth, discarding the contents of the strainer. Skim off any visible fat from the broth. Return the broth to boil on medium-high and let it boil for about 10 minutes. Add salt and pepper to taste.

FOR THE MINESTRA DI SEMOLINA:

In a medium bowl, whisk the egg and Cream of Wheat together. Add the Parmesan, milk, butter, salt, and pepper and whisk well to combine. The mixture should be the consistency of thick pancake batter. Add more milk, a bit at a time, if the mixture is too thick.

Heat a medium nonstick skillet over medium heat. Pour the batter into the pre-heated skillet, making one even layer. Cook for 1 minute, reduce the heat to low, and continue cooking for 4 minutes longer, until the pancake has become firm throughout. Gently flip the pancake and cook for 3 minutes longer. Remove the pancake from the skillet and let cool. Cut into $\frac{1}{4}$-inch pieces.

PUTTING IT ALL TOGETHER:

Serve the broth garnished with the minestra di semolina as a first course. Then serve the reserved meats and vegetables with the green sauce and Tuscan red sauce.

Serves 8.

Green Sauce

1/2 small red onion, peeled and finely chopped
1/3 cup packed parsley, finely chopped
2 small cornichon pickles
1 clove garlic
1 tablespoon finely chopped green bell pepper

2 tablespoons capers
black pepper
crushed red pepper
olive oil
red wine vinegar

Combine the onion, parsley, cornichons, garlic, bell pepper, and capers in a food processor and pulse just until everything is well chopped but not pureed. Add small amounts of black pepper, crushed red pepper, olive oil, and vinegar to taste, pulsing to incorporate them well.

NOTE: This recipe can be doubled or tripled to make as much green sauce as you need.

Makes about 1/2 cup green sauce.

Tuscan Red Sauce

2 cloves garlic
2 cups flat-leaf parsley leaves
1/4 cup olive oil

1/4 cup tomato paste dissolved in 1 cup water
salt
pepper

Mince the garlic and parsley together. In a medium saucepan, heat the oil on high heat until very hot but not smoking. Add the garlic-parsley mixture and cook, tossing occasionally, for about 1 minute. Add the dissolved tomato paste. Stir the sauce constantly until it begins to thicken. Remove from the heat. Season to taste with salt and pepper.

Makes about 1 cup red sauce.

Riso alla Marinara *(Rice with Shellfish)*

RICE IS ONE OF THOSE THINGS, like pizza, that everyone assumes Italians eat all the time. Actually in the North we didn't see much of this import from southern Italy, where rice is grown, until about forty years ago. It was one of the early Italian home-cooking dishes that we put on the menu at Le Cirque and it has never come off.

1 ½ cups rice

1 pound littleneck clams, soaked in cold water for 2 hours and well drained

½ pound small shrimp, peeled and deveined

3 medium zucchini, coarsely chopped

1 clove garlic, minced

⅓ cup olive oil

1 tablespoon coarsely chopped fresh parsley

½ cup white wine

½ teaspoon curry powder

salt

pepper

Cook the rice according to the package directions, and set aside.

In a medium saucepan, steam the clams briefly in fresh water, just until they open. Remove the clams from the pan and set aside. (If any of the clams refuse to open, discard them.) Strain the water the clams steamed in and set aside.

In a large skillet, heat the olive oil over medium-high heat. Add the shrimp, zucchini, and garlic and cook just until the shrimp are bright orange and white and opaque. Add the parsley and cook for 1 minute. Add the white wine and the reserved clam liquid and cook for 1 minute. Stir in the curry and the cooked rice. Remove from the heat, and mix well. Season with salt and pepper to taste. Add the clams, and serve immediately.

Serves 6.

Risotto with Vegetables

OUR CUSTOMERS love the special risotto we make in white truffle season, but there is no getting away from the fact that white truffles are not for the home budget. Still there are as many ways to add flavor to a risotto as there are ways to make pasta. Risotto is a great dish when you want to get kids to eat vegetables. My boys always loved my risotto with peas or asparagus. You can also use radicchio, fennel, onions, mushrooms: The list is as long as your imagination and creativity.

$^1/_2$ cup olive oil

1 large white onion, finely chopped

1 carrot, peeled and finely cubed

1 small stalk celery, finely chopped

$^1/_2$ cup chopped pancetta

$1\,^1/_2$ pounds fresh fava beans (or any other fresh or frozen broad beans)

2 zucchini cut into large cubes

$^1/_4$ cup finely chopped fresh parsley

1 tablespoon finely chopped fresh basil

1 pound arborio rice (about 2 cups)

1 chicken bouillon cube

1 quart hot water

$^2/_3$ cup grated Parmesan cheese

2 tablespoons butter

salt

pepper

In a large saucepan, heat the olive oil over high heat. Add the onion, carrot, celery, and pancetta and cook for 2 to 3 minutes. Reduce the heat to medium and cook until the onions begin to soften and the pancetta begins to brown, 7 to 10 minutes. Increase the heat to medium-high and add the fava, zucchini, parsley, and basil and cook for 2 minutes, stirring frequently. Add the rice, and cook, stirring, for 2 minutes until the rice is well coated with the oil.

Add the bouillon cube, and slowly add 1 cup of the hot water. Decrease the heat to medium and cook, stirring constantly, until the water has been fully absorbed. Stir in the remaining hot water $^1/_2$ cup at a time, making sure the previous addition has been absorbed before adding more. It takes about 25 minutes to add all the water and cook the rice.

Remove the rice from the heat and add $^1/_2$ cup of the Parmesan and the butter, stirring until the butter has melted. Season with salt and pepper to taste. Transfer to a serving bowl. Put the cooked clams on top. Sprinkle the remaining Parmesan on top. Serve immediately.

Serves 6 to 8.

Risotto Tri-Colore

As you may have guessed by now, I am very proud of my Italian heritage. This risotto has the three colors of the Italian flag: red, green and white. I first made it when I wanted something that really looked dramatic for the Regis and Kathy Lee show.

Red Sauce and Green Sauce
$^{1}/_{3}$ cup tomato puree
1 small clove garlic
2 tablespoons olive oil
$^{1}/_{4}$ cup water
$^{1}/_{2}$ cup cooked spinach

Risotto
$^{1}/_{4}$ cup olive oil
1 medium white onion, finely chopped
1 $^{3}/_{4}$ cups arborio rice
$^{1}/_{2}$ cup white wine
1 quart hot chicken stock or broth

$^{1}/_{4}$ pound Parmesan cheese, grated (about 1 $^{1}/_{3}$ cups), plus more for serving
1 stick (4 ounces) butter, cut into small pieces

FOR THE RED SAUCE:
In a food processor, puree the tomato, garlic, and olive oil together. In a small skillet, bring the puree to boil. Add the water and simmer, stirring constantly, until it thickens. Remove from the heat and set aside.

FOR THE GREEN SAUCE:
Squeeze any excess water from the spinach. Puree the spinach in a food processor.

FOR THE RISOTTO:
In a large saucepan, heat the olive oil over medium heat. Add the onion and cook just until soft and translucent, do not brown it. Add the rice and cook, stirring, for 2 minutes until the rice is well coated with the oil. Add the wine slowly. Cook, stirring constantly, until the wine has evaporated. Begin to stir in the hot stock, about $^{1}/_{2}$ cup at a time, making sure the previous addition has been absorbed before adding more. It takes about 25 minutes to add all the stock and cook the rice. When fully cooked, remove from the heat and add the Parmesan and butter. Stir until the butter is melted and thoroughly combined with the rice.

Place one third of the risotto in the center of a serving tray. Mix the red sauce with the second part of the risotto and place it alongside the white rice. Mix the green sauce with the third part of the risotto, and place it on the other side of the white rice.

Sprinkle additional Parmesan on top, if desired. Serve immediately.

Serves 4.

Thirty-Vegetable Soup

THIS IS A TRADITIONAL DISH that you learn from your grandmother. Among the old ladies there is always a little contest for who can claim the most vegetables in the soup. Some say they put thirty-two. Some say forty. Basically it requires whatever you have around. The important thing is lots of beans and potatoes.

Customers at Circo often ask me, "Are there really thirty vegetables?"

"Of course," I answer, "Count them. If there aren't thirty there you can bring your complaint to me. "

Bean puree

3 cups dried cannellini (Great Northern) beans (about 1 pound)

4 quarts water

2 tablespoons dried sage leaves

2 tablespoons dried rosemary

2 tablespoons dried thyme

2 tablespoons dried basil

2 tablespoons dried parsley

Thirty vegetables

1 small celery root, peeled and diced

1 bulb fennel, halved, core removed, finely chopped

$^1/_2$ butternut squash, diced

1 turnip, peeled and diced

$^1/_2$ head of broccoli, cut into small pieces (about $^3/_4$ cup)

1 small bunch broccoli rabe, cut into small pieces (about 1 cup)

1 bunch kale, coarsely chopped (about 1 $^1/_2$ cups)

6 plum tomatoes, cut into small pieces

1 large baking potato, peeled and diced

2 leeks, well cleaned and sliced crosswise

1 zucchini, halved lengthwise and thinly sliced crosswise

1 yellow squash, halved lengthwise and thinly sliced crosswise

1 small yellow onion, peeled and finely chopped

1 small white onion, peeled and finely chopped

1 small red onion, peeled and finely chopped

1 Yukon Gold potato, peeled and diced

2 stalks celery, thinly sliced

1 large carrot, peeled and sliced into rounds

5 scallions, coarsely chopped

1 large artichoke heart, sliced

1 cup peas

1 cup 1-inch asparagus pieces

1 cup green beans, cut into small pieces

1 cup julienned green cabbage

1 cup julienned Chinese (Napa) cabbage

1 cup julienned black cabbage (also called Tuscan kale or cavalo nero)

2 tablespoons minced garlic

2 cups green Swiss chard, coarsely chopped

2 cups red Swiss chard, coarsely chopped

2 cups cleaned spinach leaves, coarsely chopped

salt

pepper

(recipe continued on page 164)

FOR THE BEAN PUREE:

Soak the cannellini beans overnight in two quarters of the water. Drain and put the beans in a large saucepan with the remaining water and herbs. Bring to a boil. Then reduce the heat and simmer for 1 hour, until the beans are very soft. Add the tomatoes and simmer for 10 minutes longer. Remove from the heat and let cool for 10 minutes. Puree in a blender (a few cups at a time).

FOR THE THIRTY VEGETABLES:

In a very large pot, combine the bean puree and all the remaining vegetables except the Swiss chard and spinach. Season with salt and pepper to taste and simmer until all the vegetables are soft but not mushy, 20 to 30 minutes. Add the Swiss chard and the spinach and cook for 2 minutes. Serve hot.

NOTE: Serve with croutons and a drizzle of extra-virgin olive oil on each serving.

Serves 8 to 10.

Fried Pumpkin Ravioli

ONE YEAR Martha Stewart wanted a Thanksgiving story about my family. I am often asked to create a Tuscan Thanksgiving—which of course makes me smile because we have no such holiday in Tuscany. I guess the idea is a big family meal, and we Tuscans have big families and big meals, so why not? This recipe is a basic crispy fried ravioli filled with pumpkin in honor of the season.

Ravioli dough

1 cup all-purpose flour
2 egg yolks
2 tablespoons butter, softened
2 tablespoons milk
1 tablespoon sugar
1 tablespoon Sambuca
zest of $1/4$ lemon

Filling

$1/2$ cup canned pumpkin
$1/2$ cup ricotta cheese
$1/4$ cup sugar
2 Amaretti cookies, finely crushed
$1/2$ teaspoon vanilla

vegetable oil, for frying
$1/4$ cup confectioners' sugar, for sprinkling

FOR THE RAVIOLI DOUGH:
Combine all of the ingredients in a food processor and process to make a soft dough. Transfer the dough to a small bowl and let sit, covered, for 1 hour.

FOR THE FILLING:
In a large bowl, beat together all of the ingredients until thoroughly combined.

ASSEMBLING THE RAVIOLI:
Using a rolling pin or pasta machine, make two long sheets from the ravioli dough about 4 inches wide and $1/4$-inch thick (much thicker than regular pasta). Place heaping teaspoonfuls of the filling down the center of one sheet of the pasta, spacing them approximately 1 inch from the end of the sheet and 2 inches apart. Cover this sheet of pasta with the other sheet, and gently press it down between the mounds of filling. Cut the pasta between each mound of filling and then press the edges of each ravioli firmly closed with your fingers or the tines of a fork.

Preheat the vegetable oil in a pot or deep fryer. Deep fry the ravioli in the oil, in batches, just until they turn pale golden brown. Remove from the oil and sprinkle them immediately with confectioners' sugar. Serve warm or cold.

Serves 4.

Cenci (Fritters)

ALTHOUGH EVERYBODY makes these fried-dough bows in Tuscany, the very best were made by the mother of Alessandro Giuntolli, our first chef at Circo and the husband of my niece, Mirella. We make them for Carnivale, what Americans call Fat Tuesday. It signifies the beginning of Lent. Right after the war, on this holiday, I remember seeing my first *pintoraccia*— kind of like a Mexican piñata. They would put these up in the town square and the children would take turns swinging at it until it broke and all the candies inside would come out.

3 tablespoons butter, softened
2 tablespoons sugar
1 lemon, zest of (about $\frac{1}{2}$ teaspoon)
3 egg yolks
2 tablespoons milk

2 tablespoons Sambuca (anise-flavored liqueur)
$1\frac{1}{2}$ tablespoons vanilla extract
$2\frac{1}{2}$ cups all-purpose flour
vegetable oil for deep frying
$\frac{1}{4}$ cup confectioners' sugar

Combine the butter, sugar, and lemon zest in a food processor. Add the egg yolks, one at a time, pulsing to combine well after each. Add the milk, Sambuca, and vanilla. Mix well. Add the flour. Combine well until you have a soft and crumbly dough. Add a few drops of milk if the dough is too dry.

Roll out the dough into a rectangle 8 inches wide and $\frac{1}{8}$-inch thick. Cut the dough into 8- x 1-inch strips, using a knife or a pastry wheel. Carefully twist the strips into loose knots. Deep fry the knots in hot oil until they just begin to turn golden brown. Remove from oil to paper towels. Sprinkle immediately and abundantly with confectioners' sugar. Serve warm.

Serves 4.

Crème Caramel

I HAVE no stronger food memory than that of my Aunt Livia's crème caramel. Of all of us back in the old country, she was the one professional cook. Before she moved to Rome she cooked for a local member of the nobility. When the count and his wife died, they left Livia the keys to the house and everything in it. Of course once the relatives got wind of this they came in and took most of it, but Livia ended up with a lot of beautiful things including a wonderful little porcelain statue of a man holding a flower. Livia moved in with us and made the best hot chocolate, always letting me lick the pot. And then there was her crème caramel! She made it on top of the stove in a double boiler. To caramelize it she would put the lid on it and place charcoal on top of the lid. Ancient technology, but it was delicious!

6 cups whole milk

1 large strip orange zest

1 large strip lemon zest

1 vanilla bean or 1 teaspoon vanilla extract

12 egg yolks

1 1/2 cups sugar

In a large saucepan, bring the milk to a boil over medium-high heat. Add the orange zest, lemon zest, and vanilla bean, if using. Reduce the heat to medium, and cook, stirring frequently, until the volume of the milk has been reduced by half, about 30 minutes.

Strain the milk through cheesecloth into a medium bowl, pressing it to extract the flavors from the citrus zests and the vanilla. Discard the contents of the cheesecloth. Add the egg yolks and 3/4 cup sugar (and the vanilla extract, if using) to the reduced milk. Stir gently to combine the ingredients well, but do not whip or beat it. (Try not to create any bubbles in the milk mixture.) Set aside.

Preheat oven to 350 F. Pull out a 9- or 10-inch soufflé dish, and have it ready (do not grease).

Put the remaining 3/4 cup sugar into a large, nonstick skillet over medium-high heat and cook, stirring occasionally, until the sugar has melted. Pour it immediately into the bottom of the soufflé dish, tilting the pan to make sure the entire bottom gets coated. (Work fast because the sugar will harden quickly.) Pour the reduced milk mixture over the caramelized sugar in the soufflé pan. Set aside.

Place a small, folded kitchen towel in the bottom of a large baking pan. Carefully place the filled soufflé dish on top of the towel in the pan, and pour about 1 inch of boiling water around the dish. Place the entire bain marie into the preheated oven, and bake for 1 $\frac{1}{2}$ hours, until a toothpick inserted in the center comes out dry.

Remove the crème caramel from the bain marie. Let cool for about 20 minutes. Then cover, refrigerate to cool completely, at least 2 hours.

When ready to serve, turn out the crème caramel onto a serving platter, and drizzle with any of the syrupy caramel from the bottom of the pan. Serve immediately.

Serves 8.

Index